The RAYMOND TINSLEY Story
Get Up On The Hook

Willie Hoskins

Printed in the United States of America

Wilhos Publishing
An Educational Publisher
P.O. Box 42369
Houston, Texas 77242

Copyright © 2011 Willie Edward Hoskins
All rights reserved. No part of this book may be reproduced or transmitted in any form or by any means electrical or mechanical, including photocopying, recording, or by an information storage and retrieval system, except of classroom use, without permission in writing from the publisher.

ISBN: 0966668308
ISBN-13: 9780966668308

THIS BOOK IS THE PROPERTY OF:			
STATE _____		BOOK NO. _____	
PROVINCE _____			
COUNTY _____			
PARISH _____			
SCHOOL DISTRICT _____			
OTHER _____			
			CONDITION
ISSUED TO	YEAR USED	ISSUED	RETURNED

PUPILS TO WHOM THIS TEXTBOOK IS ISSUED MUST NOT WRITE ON ANY PAGE OR MARK ANY PART OF IT IN ANY WAY. CONSUMABLE TEXTBOOKS EXCEPTED.

1. TEACHERS SHOULD SEE THAT THE PUPIL'S NAME IS CLEARLY WRITTEN IN INK IN THE SPACES ABOVE IN EVERY BOOK ISSUED.
2. THE FOLLOWING SHOULD BE USED IN RECORDING THE CONDITION OF THE BOOK: NEW; GOOD; FAIR BAD.

About The Author

During my summer vacation from my teaching position at Pinkston High School, I would visit my mother in Chicago. Pinkston was one of *Dallas Independent School District* High Schools located in west Dallas. The school was across the street from a federal project; a low poverty, high crime community of mostly single parents with a high drop out rate and teen pregnancy.

During my stay at Pinkston, the student enrollment was 90% afro-American. Mexican American enrollment increased dramatically, and so did gang activities and social issues in the community. I recall on one occasion a rival gang fired shots into the bus carrying band members. One of the shots shattered the bus window close to where I was seated. This had been a challenging year and I was definitely ready for my summer vacation. I wrote about my teaching experience at Pinkston High School in my Auto Biography titled *"Soulful Sounds of Survival."* I went into hibernation the first week of my vacation and planned my trip to Chicago.

Mother was a dialysis patient and had to be transported to the center two days a week by paramedics. My sister was also a dialysis patient and was on the waiting list for a liver transplant. She never spoke of the liver transplant to me. After a month of following their dialysis treatment schedule, I concluded that it would be difficult for her to manage her illness and mom. I flew back to Dallas and requested an emergency one year leave of absence from *Dallas Independent School District.* In August of 1989, I moved to Chicago.

All of my sisters lived on the west side with the exception of my oldest sister who was taking care of mother. The Hoskins family moved from Memphis, Tennessee to Chicago, Illinois during my junior year in college. I was hesitant about staying with my sister because of our childhood Experiences. The two of us never got along. She had a mean streak in her which made it difficult for me to like her. But, I had to learn to live with her because of mother. I devoted two chapters in my Auto-Biography titled *"Soulful Sounds of Survival"* describing my childhood experiences while growing up with my mean sister.

The year passed quickly as I monitored mother and my sister's health. I eventually resigned from Dallas Independent School District and applied for a teaching position with *Chicago Public Schools.*

In the summer of 1990, I attended several job fairs and interviews with principals. I had an impressive resume dating back to my teaching experiences in Los Angeles, California. I wrote about my California teaching experiences in *South-Central Los Angeles* in my Auto-Biography titled *"Soulful Sounds of Survival."*

The last day of the job fair I was interviewed by the principal of **Michele Clark Middle School.** I was impressed with the goals she had set for her students and how they would be accomplished. She emphasized how vital enrichment programs were at her school and how they are *integrated into the school's academic curriculum.* An instrumental music program would be another component used to address some of the social issues of at risk and troubled kids. She also stated she had the funds to implement the program. The school received a $40,000 fine arts grant which had not been used. She wanted to start the instrumental music program by October. She granted my request to begin ordering instruments and equipment needed to start the program. I accepted the position and prepared for my first year teaching in Chicago.

Ironically, the school was located in the heart of the hood on the west side where my sisters and their kids resided. I talked with my sister and some of my *gang banging* nephews who would attend Michele Clark Middle School in September. *I explained to them they are never to call me "Uncle Willie" at school. They all agreed.*

I eventually moved to Oak Park, a small suburban city on the west side after mother passed. I hated the daily commute on the Dan Ryan Expressway from the south side to work, especially after snow and a hard freeze. During the first three months of school, I recruited kids for the instrumental music program. There were three different gang factions attending the school. Each faction was boys and girls who lived on the same block and hung out together. However, this bounty didn't last long; they eventually adopted a name that would establish there presence in the community. While waiting for the new instruments and equipment to arrive, I met with students and parents wishing to be in the program. An agreement was signed by the parent, student, principal and I outlining the rules of engagement in the instrumental music program.

<u>The rule of no gang activities during school hours was strictly enforced. Kids were immediately dropped from the program for non compliance.</u> The popularity of the program grew rapidly. The music coming from the band room characterized their Hip Hop culture; I arranged music for the band to play taken from the top R&B play list of the number one radio station in Chicago.

My experience in writing and arranging music dates back to my California experiences during my short stay in the entertainment industry. I wrote about my California experience in the entertainment business in my Auto-Biography titled **"Soulful Sounds of Survival."**

Students were eager to join the program. Some were placed on the waiting list. Participating students knew they would immediately be replaced if dropped from the program. Gang activities decreased rapidly. The group was invited to perform for city and local events. City officials visited our school and participated in local parades. I later added an all girl drill team and flags to the performing group. **(Pictures are available)**

The success of the instrumental music program popularity expanded throughout the community. The band and drill team combined performances attracted large audiences. I formed a cluster with the local elementary and High School. The local high school band instructor praised my efforts and supported my program. Many continued their music education in the high school band. I later learned some received music scholarships to Black Colleges.

Why I Wrote the Raymond Tinsley Story

Very valuable experiences I truly remember were the Michele Clark Middle School Family Retreat. It was mandatory for employees, including teacher aides, cafeteria workers, janitors, and voluntary for parents and community leaders to attend. One of the three day retreats was held at an exquisite country club. After an early dismissal on Friday, all employees reported to the country club for the three day workshop. After checking in and enjoying the sites, we attended a five star dinner. Man! It was hard to choose from a variety of American and Mediterranean dishes in the buffet line. Entertainment was also provided.

However, this bounty didn't last long; we were up early the next morning focusing on the planned agenda. The agenda included topics of improving test scores and addressing the social and emotional problems of at risk and troubled adolescents. Five committees were formed addressing the problem areas. The groups rotated addressing all problem areas. The objective was to come out of the retreat with solutions to these problems. After a thirty minute break for lunch, we were back to work discussing and searching for new ideas to improve student's academic performance. The Better Boys Club of Chicago heard about the success of the instrumental music program at the school. The club conducted after school programs for kids living in high crime areas daily from 4:00 p.m. to 7:00 p.m. I volunteered my services each Thursday after school.

One evening after leaving the club, local weather reports predicted a blizzard snow and ice storm was headed for Chicago. Twenty to twenty two inches of snow was predicted with temperatures hovering in the teens, and a wind chill factor of minus three degrees. All Suburban and Chicago Schools will be closed on Friday. I knew this was a serious warning because Chicago Public Schools do not close because of snow. A mayoral candidate won an election because of her planning and preparation for preventing the city not to shut down. It was a big issue in the next election.

I stopped at the closest store on the way home and purchased food and essentials needed for a four day lock down. When I reached home, the red light message button on the phone was blinking. One of the calls was from one of my sisters. My nine year old niece answered the phone speaking incoherently trying to inform me that Jonathan, my sister's oldest boy, had been shot in a drive by. They were at Loretta St. Hospital and wanted me to come as soon as possible. I dropped the bags of grocery and promptly headed to hospital. I knew the exact location of the hospital because I traveled this route to work each morning. On my arrival, I was directed to the emergency room where doctors were working feverishly on Jonathan's wounds.

Distraught, sadly distressed and a heavy heart, my sister had to be moved from the area. Jonathan's friends were waiting for an update of his condition in the waiting room. I knew some of the kids in the room because of their participation in the instrumental music program at the school. I knew something was going down after this act of violence by looking in their solemn and revengeful faces. Without a doubt, there was going to be retaliation against the persons responsible for this act of violence. Before leaving the hospital,

I talked briefly with Nathan. Nathan was one of the kids I started in my instrumental music program. He was now a senior and had a music scholarship to Grambling University. I was hoping this kid would make the right decision and not become a part of retaliatory teen violence.

The blustering snow and howling wind paralyzed vehicles along the way when driving home. I safely arrived home after spinning my way through the blinding snow. The thoughts of what happened to Jonathan weighed heavily on my mind. Snowed in for four days and living like a hermit, I began writing ***The Raymond Tinsley Story.***

Overview

The Raymond Tinsley Story focuses on the social and emotional problems of troubled adolescents growing up and attending inner-city schools. This book provides workbook activities that will help students improve reading skills and assists students in applying skills and strategies needed to pass city, state, and standardized national tests. Survival and dealing with every day social issues in the community impedes academic growth. The Tinsley series provides solutions to many of these problems. Some of the problems fall into these categories: Peer pressure-Conflict with parents-Gang influence and affiliation-Bullying-Alcohol and Drugs-Crime-Guns-Sexually Transmitted Diseases-Education and Teen Pregnancy.

The Tinsley series is divided into short chapters that can be easily read and understood. The chapters are divided into five units. Each unit follows a logical plan to improve comprehension, vocabulary, writing and test taking skills. While the book tries to provide a model of good grammar and enhanced vocabulary, colloquial English and slang are also used throughout the book. This is done when such language is deemed appropriate to the characters and to create a mood. Some of these passages of informal English are underlined for discussion.

Chapters 1-4 (Unit I) are action chapters. Each chapter ends in a drama situation, and creates anticipation of reading the next chapter. The action chapters immediately capture the attention of readers, and leave them curious as to how the main character, Raymond, will prepare himself Psychologically for the championship game knowing his coach was wounded in a drive-by shooting and he has now become player-coach in tomorrow's championship game. How will he react to Benny D., the psychotic drug dealer who is out to sabotage the game? Some of the action chapters in Unit 1 include:

- A drive-by shooting at the school
- A fight between three rival cheer leaders from Carver High School and two cheer leaders from Martin Luther King High School
- Raymond's stepfather is mugged by Benny D., the psychotic drug dealer who is frantically trying to sabotage the championship game.

STUDENTS MUST COMPLETE UNIT I, INCLUDING ALL WORKBOOK ACTIVITIES BEFORE PROCEEDING TO UNIT II

Here are some suggestions for reading assignments for students to fully digest the story and workbook activities.

- Assign Unit I (Chapters 1-4). After students read Unit I, allow them to work in their journals on workbook activities.
- Require students to purchase an 8 x 11 inch spiral notebook to record their findings. Answers in their journal should follow the same format as in Workbook activities.
- Permit students to research answers by reviewing the previous chapters.
- Assist students when researching the answers and writing them in their journals. This activity prepares them for the Unit I test.

Unit I test is a compilation of Chapters 1-4. In your grade book, record student scores for each workbook activity. Label each chapter. Students should be graded on neatness and well kept journals for each workbook activity. Follow this procedure for each unit. Post grades on a roster chart. *<u>The goal of The Raymond Tinsley Story is to communicate to adolescents the fun of reading and the importance of reading in helping them to become active and productive members of society.</u>*

The Tinsley series is designed to develop critical thinking skills that help at-risk adolescents think through decisions and choices they must make during this crucial time in their lives.

Willie Hoskins

The Raymond Tinsley Story

Chapter Highlights

Chapter I
Senior projects • you can't deny me my rapping rights • Spraying the campus with automatic assault weapons • the coach is hit twice

Chapter II
The Rush to Somerset Memorial Hospital • the challenge from Coach Mickey • Player-coach accepts the responsibility

Chapter III
Tigers on the loose • Have you seen my teeth? I need my teeth to eat my beef *Throwing down at Slap Burgers

Chapter IV
He had seen that look before • He knew something was about to go down • Seven young brothers were killed.. • The HIV virus, 20% increase among high school students

Chapter V
Evelyn (Dee)—a crack user • her friend Latisha • we're just hanging out trying to make something happen • Milton finds the kids in the bedroom playing with a cigarette lighter

Chapter VI
An attempt to destroy the game plan • the criminally insane drug dealer • Bennie D., wanted by the police

Chapter VII
The morning workout • A mother's wish • the jamming pep rally • Two funky tunes by the MLK band • the red plastic covering the exit sign shatters and falls to the floor

Chapter VIII
Michael Jordan Park • Cassandra Hawkins, fine and smart • NBA dreams • the new frontier • the judicial system

Chapter IX
This smoke will have you jumping over The Hook • The Eddie Murphy and Martin Lawrence Show • A case of amnesia • the big surprise • the winning lottery ticket

Chapter X
New uniforms • Police escort to the Coliseum • the starting five

Chapter XI
The tip off • passing the ball with accuracy • Raymond and Clarence: two tall trees reaching for the ceiling!

Chapter XII
The big chase • the capture of Benny D. • the five second play-Scholarship recipients

Chapter XIII
Getting ready for UCLA • The California rap • It's party time • we would never do anything to blow our scholarships • the lethal salad fork • Watery red eyes and slow speech make it obvious • Ebony girls on the beach

Chapter XIV
When they kissed, two little girls behind them said "Stop that!"

Chapter XV
The Prevention and Intervention program at the park

Chapter XVI
The drive to California • the Interstate showdown in Arizona • Slap Burgers, 52 miles ahead, Exit 27A

Chapter XVII
An official apology from the City of Flagstaff • Flagstaff adopts prevention and intervention model program from Chicago • the co-ed dormitory • Milton falls asleep with his ear to the wall • Raymond falls asleep thinking about his first night on a college campus

Chapter XVIII
The drive-through registration • Raymond knows he has to go to another level of play to run with this team • Visible gang signs on abandoned buildings • R.T., The five-second play • A breathless moment for Cal State fans

Chapter XIX
The boys return to Chicago for the summer • More about the prevention and intervention program • A clinic conducted by athletes from the NBA • A dialogue with gang bangers, NBA athletes, college athletes, and community leaders • the boys from Chicago out swim sharks

Chapter XX
The five-year, $120 million dollar contract with the Chicago Bulls • "I may have contracted the HIV virus"

Prologue

At first, it was difficult for Raymond to understand why the drive-by shooting happened the day before the championship game. Was this just another random shooting between rival gangs intended to hurt innocent students, or was it a ploy to throw Martin Luther King High School Basketball team off of their game? There were a lot of questions to be answered before the team could "psych" itself up to the level of play needed to win the championship game.

This is the story of Raymond Tinsley, star center for Martin Luther King High School's Basketball Team. Raymond has to walk through the pitfalls of drugs, teen violence, peer pressure, gang banging and social problems in the community before fulfilling his dreams of playing ball in college and becoming a superstar in the NBA.

His greatest dream was to return to the community after college and help adolescents like him fulfill their dreams. The Raymond Tinsley story realistically portrays the lifestyle of adolescents' transition from elementary to middle school or junior high, and then a second transition to high school. These transitions bring many risks and opportunities to make decisions—for better or worse. Unfortunately, the worse decisions could prove to be fatal when they result in gang banging and similar reactions.

The Raymond Tinsley story is a timely story and will help adolescents think through decisions and choices they must make during this crucial time in their lives.

Willie Hoskins

Chapter One

Senior projects
You can't deny me my rapping rights
Spraying the campus with automatic assault weapons

The Coach is hit twice

Raymond Tinsley, the 6'9" star center for Martin Luther King High School's basket ball team tried to remain calm during his fifth period English IV class. Mr. Williams was encumbering the class with required assignments for seniors prior to graduation. Walking over to the desk where Raymond was seated, he completed his explanation of the assignment.

"Senior Projects are due the first week in May," he stated, while walking over to the window, and watching the traffic move slowly through the school zone. "I would like to personally wish the best of luck to the Martin Luther King High basketball team in tomorrow's championship game," he added, while walking back to the front of the classroom.

"Yo, Boy!" shouted one of the students jumping up from his desk and giving the victory sign. "GET UP ON THE HOOK. GET UP ON THE HOOK," was echoed in unison from members of the class. After class, Raymond and two members of the team stood in the hallway. They talked about The Hook and personal strategies on how they thought they could stop his lethal hook shot.

The Hook was Clarence Johnson. Clarence Johnson was a senior and star center for Carver High School basketball team. It was almost impossible to stop his hook shot. Coaches from major colleges and universities had scouted Clarence since his freshman year. Clarence had visited several of the institutions but had not decided which he would attend. Ninety-six percent of his hook shots would find their way through the nets. Raymond, the team, the coach, the school, and the community knew that The Hook had to be stopped if there was any chance of their winning the championship game "Yo, Milton, let's make practice, brother. You know Coach Mickey is a little tense about our last practice before the game," Raymond said.

"All right, I hear you R.T.," Milton answered reluctantly. Milton has stopped one of the girls in the hall, and was seriously trying to get her phone number. Milton and Raymond had played ball together since their freshman year at King High School.

"Hey, Milton," Raymond called out to him again.

"All right, I hear you," he replied, but continued talking to the girl.

Eric Malone, another senior on the team walked up and asked Raymond

"What's going on?"

"Nothing, really, I am trying to convince the player that we are due in Coach Mickey's office, like right now. This is the third girl he has fallen in love with today," Raymond jokingly replied.

"Maybe he needs a little friendly physical persuasion," Eric answered. The two boys walked over to Milton. Each grabbed one of his arms. They lifted him off the floor and began moving him in the direction of Coach Mickey's office. He struggled as he pretended to work his way out of the grip of Raymond and Eric. The girl began laughing and so did everyone in the hall who saw what was going on.

"Unhand me, you can't deny me my rapping rights! She loves me—me! Can't you see that?" Milton hollered. Raymond and Eric continued moving Milton in the direction of Coach Mickey's office.

Coach Mickey was a graduate of Grambling State University. He had been the basketball coach at King High for twenty-one years. He played professional ball for two years but was forced to stop after a serious knee injury. The school had won seven state championships since he began coaching at King High School. Several colleges had offered him coaching positions, but he was dedicated to coach high school ball because the need was so great to influence young black athletes to continue their education after high school.

When the boys arrived at his office, they found Coach Mickey on the basketball court doing imaginary defensive moves under the basket. "What's up coach,?" Raymond asked. "Hey fellows, come on over," he answered while quickly passing the ball to Raymond. "I think I have a solution for stopping Clarence Johnson's shot. Let's go to my office and look at the video of our last game with Carver."

The four watched five minutes of the first half. The coach turned to Raymond and said. "See what's up, Raymond? Clarence clearly signals when he is going to hook.

Notice how his left foot pivots. Then he takes a long stride with his right foot to position himself for the hook shot. What you have to do during the long stride is position yourself and time the shot for his release. Better still, let's go out to the court, and I will show you where I'm coming from."

On the court under the basket, Coach Mickey positioned himself as Clarence Johnson had in the video. Raymond positioned himself defensively behind the coach. Milton and Eric watched attentively as the coach and Raymond demonstrated the moves. The three boys knew that they had to stop The Hook if there were any chance of their winning the game. "Notice the stride of my right foot as I attempt the hook shot. When he is taking the slow stride, his right arm is extended away from his opponent. Timing it carefully, if you can get in front of Clarence, your chances of stopping his shot increases dramatically," Coach Mickey said.

Suddenly! A volley of gun shots was heard from the outside. "What's up? What's up? What's up? Milton shouted out several times.

"I don't know. I don't know." Coach Mickey replied. "Let's check it out."

The coach and the boys rushed out of the gym, through the hall, to the side exit doors. The four hit the side door exits simultaneously. On the outside, they saw a car speeding toward them headed southwest on 69th Street. Automatic weapons were pointed out the window.

"Down coach!" Raymond screamed out.

Tat, tat, tat, tat, tat! The sound of assault weapons rang out in a terrifying echo. They tried to take cover behind whatever was closest to them. Milton found cover behind the bronze statue of Martin Luther King in the center pathway leading to the entrance. Ding, ding, ding-the bullets bounced off the statue. When the car was out of range, everyone returned to their feet except Coach Mickey.

"Is everybody all right, is everybody all right?" Raymond asked. "Over here, over here!" Coach Mickey cried out. "I've been hit." "What!" the boys screamed in panic

Activities

Understanding what you have read.
Do not write in this book. Use your Raymond Tinsley journal.

PART I. True/False

1. Senior projects were due the first week in June.
2. Clarence Johnson was known for his jump shot.
3. The Hook had to be stopped; if there was any chance of their winning the Championship game.
4. The coach told Raymond he had to develop his own strategy on how the Hook should be guarded.
5. The speeding car with automatic weapons was headed south on 79th Street.
6. "Down, coach!" Milton screamed out when the shooting started.
7. Raymond took cover behind the bronze statue of Martin Luther King.
8. Eric cried out, "I've been hit."

PART II *Know Your Characters*

Match the description on the left, with the proper characters below

1. The boy rapping to the girl in the hall
2. The teammate that helped Raymond escort Milton to the gym
3. The 6'9' senior basketball star for Martin Luther King High School
4. The basketball coach
5. The 7'1 senior basketball star for Carver H.S

A. Raymond
B. Clarence
C. Coach Mickey
D. Milton
E. Eric

PART III Questions to Discuss
Describe

A. How you think the boys felt after the drive-by?
B. What should be done about the shooting?
1. Seek revenge.

2. Give the police a chance to arrest the person (s) responsible.
3. Discuss it with the team.
4. Do nothing.
5. Other.
Give a full explanation of the choices you select along with the possible consequences of each.

PART IV: *Vocabulary*
A. Use a dictionary to find the definition for the words listed below. Report your findings to the class. Explain how each was used in Chapter 1.
B. Construct a new sentence for each word'

Assignment	dramatically
opponent	solution
Assault weapon	encumbered
influence	strategies
Bronze	escort
persuasion	statue
Community	imaginary
pivot	stride
Demonstrate	institutions
required	volley

PART V. Writing Prompts

Select *one of the following for your homework assignment.*

Homework assignments should not be included in your Raymond Tinsley journal. These assignments should be given to your teacher upon completion. Other information to help you with your writing assignments sill be included from time to time. Use these tips for future writing assignments.

   A. Write, describing how you think the boys felt after the drive-by shooting.
   B. What should be done about the drive-by shooting? (Class Discussion)
Give the police a chance to arrest the persons responsible.
   1. Discuss it with the team.
   2. Seek revenge.
   3. Other.
Give a full explanation of the choices you select along with the possible consequences of each.
   C. Raymond, the team, the coach, the school and the community knew that The Hook had to be stopped if there was any chance of their winning the Championship game. Describe your feelings if you were Raymond assigned to guard the Hook.
   D. Write your personal reaction of each character.
   1. Raymond
   2. Milton
   3. Coach Mickey

Chapter One

E. Chapter I end with Coach Mickey being wounded in the drive-by shooting. Write, describing your feelings if you were Raymond, knowing you had to accept the responsibility of being player-coach in tomorrow championship game.

Chapter Two

The Rush to Somerest Memorial Hospital
The Challenge from Coach Mickey
Player-Coach accepts the responsibility

"I'll get some help; I'll get it right away!" Milton called out, as he began running to the principal's office. When he arrived, he found out that some students had been wounded by the same gang that wounded Coach Mickey. The school's secretary told Milton they had already called for help; the sound of sirens from police, ambulances and fire trucks could be heard in a distance speeding toward Martin Luther King High School.

Milton went out in the street and directed the paramedics to the 69th Street entrance where Coach Mickey had been wounded..

Coach Mickey had been hit twice; once in the right upper thigh and a close graze on his right side. The paramedics tended Coach Mickey's wounds and immediately rushed him to Somerest Memorial Hospital which was nine blocks away.

"All students to the auditorium," was the call over the intercom by the principals of Martin Luther King High School. Students were openly crying, students were both angry and sad. Some spoke of revenge on the people responsible for this terrifying act of violence.

It didn't take long for the students to understand that this was a time for them to come together and decide what could and would be done about this act of violence. Students and staff began walking toward the front entrance to the school. They all came together in the main auditorium, all except Raymond and Eric. They rode in the ambulance with wounded Coach Mickey to Somerest Memorial Hospital.

The principal and officers assured the students they had good descriptions of the assailants and arrest warrants had been issued for their arrest. One student stood up and told the officers that an arrest had better come real soon because many of the students had other ways of dealing with the people responsible for this act of violence. After the assembly, the students were dismissed to their homeroom on lock down for the remainder of the day.

Why now, Raymond thought as the ambulance sped down 69th with the siren at maximum volume. Thank God, he thought, the coach was going to pull through this one. What about his team mates, the championship game, college, his family, and the reaction to the drive-by shooting? Will I be able to play well enough in the championship game to convince the scouts that I am worthy of a college scholarship? Many thoughts ran through his mind on the way to the hospital.

"I was wounded in the Gulf War, and I will pull through this one also," Coach Mickey said, as the doctors worked feverishly treating his wounds. "Well, Captain, Coach Mickey said, while turning to Raymond, "you gotta be player-coach in tomorrow night's championship game. The game will not be postponed because I'm not there. The game goes on."

Chapter Two

"I don't know Coach. With you not being there, the team may not be able to handle the emotion," Raymond answered.

"Come on, Raymond," Coach Mickey said, "you guys know the game plan. We have known and practiced the game-plan for tomorrow's game since the start of the season. You guys know what we have to do to win. In fact, you don't have a choice. I will not be out of here for at least a week. This horrible thing that happened to the students and me should really give you guys a reason to really play smart…and hard!" Coach Mickey said.

"I know, coach, but, but.. . ."Raymond muttered.

"But nothing, Coach Mickey interrupted. Go out there and whip some butt and bring home that trophy! Have that final practice and keep me informed. You know I'm not going anywhere for several days."

Raymond and Eric talked with concerned students and friends of Coach Mickey in the waiting room when leaving the hospital. Raymond assured the sympathizers that Coach Mickey was okay. A police car was waiting for Raymond and Eric to drive them back to school. "We have arrested three suspects, and we have a strong lead on the fourth one. Do you know a dude that goes by the name of Benny D.?" the officer asked. "Our information tells us he is a former student of Carver High School."

"I've heard the name, but I don't know much about him." Raymond answered.

"Well, we know he is a small time drug dealer, and the word is out he has a large sum of money bet on the game. We'll get him. It's just a matter of time.

You guys be careful. Watch your back. That Benny D. dude is still out there and he is desperately trying to wreck tomorrow's championship game for you guys." the officer stated.

"We know, officer, this gives us a good reason to really play well in the championship game." Raymond answered.

Arriving at the school, they headed straight for the gymnasium. When Raymond and Eric walked in, the rest of the team was in full practice.

Activities

Understanding what you have read.
Do not write in this book *Use your Raymond Tinsley journal*

PART I: *True/False*
1. Milton ran for help.
2. Raymond was out in the street to direct the first paramedics.
3. The office's secretary told Milton she had already called for help.
4. Coach Mickey had been wounded twice.
5. They immediately rushed Coach Mickey to Somerest Memorial Hospital.
6. Raymond and Eric rode in the ambulance with the coach.
7. Coach Mickey told Raymond he would be out of the hospital in time to coach the game.
8. The police had arrested three suspects and had a strong lead on the fourth shooter.
9. Benny D. was a member of the Carver High Basketball Team.
10. Coach Mickey told Raymond he should develop a game plan for the championship game.

PART II. Vocabulary Use a dictionary to find the definition of the words listed below. Construct a sentence for each word. Explain how each word was used in Chapter 2.

Assailant's	feverishly
maximum	suspects
championship	flagged
paramedics	sympathizers
desperately	graze
postponed	violence
motion	immediately
responsible	warrants

PART III Questions to Discuss
A. Why do you think the principal asked the students and teachers to assemble in the auditorium after the drive-by shooting?
B. What should Raymond say to the team in his new role as player-coach?
C. Write, describing your reactions to Benny D.

Chapter Three

Throwing down at Slap Burgers
Tigers on the loose
Have you seen my teeth? I need them to eat my beef!

After practice, Milton gave Raymond a ride to his after-school job at Slap Burgers. When they arrived, Raymond counted twelve cars in the drive-through line. Before leaving practice, Raymond had dressed in his uniform and was ready for work. He checked in with the manager, punched his time card and walked to the front counter. Raymond asked, "May I take your order, please?"

Three girls wearing Carver High School sweaters were next in line. "Hey girl," one of them shouted, "Carver is going to smoke out King Tomorrow night. In unison, the two girls loudly shouted, "I KNOW THAT'S RIGHT, THE HOOK WILL BE HOOKING!"

Raymond hesitated before speaking. He knew they were trying to intimidate him about The Hook. Again, Raymond asked, "May I have your order please!"

"Yeah, do you have the new Hook Burger?" she asked.

Again, Raymond hesitated before speaking. He was about to go-off on the three, when two cheer leaders from King High School got up in the face of the girls from Carver and asked, "Raymond, are you having a problem with these #$@@#$%@# tramps from Carver?"

"What's it to you?" one girl from Carver answered.

"Whenever you say something about King High School, it's something to me." the girl from King replied. "What do you want to do about it? We can get it on right now!"

"Bring it on, sister," the girl from Carver said.

Biff! Wham! Bam! They started fighting. One of the MLK cheerleaders was nicknamed Big Bertha. Big Bertha was BIG. She weighed 231 pounds. Big Bertha was the person at the bottom of their pyramid formation balancing 16 girls.

This act of balance and strength earned them first place in the state's cheer leaders' competition. Big Bertha was vital to the squad. Everyone respected her for her endurance and talent.

Big Bertha strong arms hooked two of the girls in a Hercules hold and banged their heads together. She sat on one girl while pulling strands of hair from the head of the other. "The setting was a nest of cats in a dog fight."

The other cheerleader from MLK high karate kicked the third girl from Carver. The girl landed on the card board statue of a man eating a Slap Burger.

"The setting was a nest of cats in a dog fight."

Raymond jumped across the counter in an attempt to break it up. The manager had already summoned security. The girls were throwing down at Slap Burgers. Raymond and the manager pulled the two girls from King off the three girls from Carver. The three girls from Carver seemed to have had enough.

Two security guards escorted them .back to their car. The arm from a sweater one of the Carver girls was wearing was completely ripped off and lying on the floor. It appeared as if a real live tiger had attacked the girls from Carver. The upper, under garment of one of the girls was torn to shreds. The human sized cardboard statue of a man eating a Slap Burger was bent all the way to the floor. It appeared to be bowing to the girls from King.

One old man lost his false teeth trying to get out of the way during the fight. He was searching for them under the table. "I can't find my teeth, I can't find my teeth. I need my teeth to eat my beef, "he kept mumbling.

The manager, Charles Davenport, said he would press no charges. The three girls from Carver sped away in an old four color 1993 Mustang whose left back fender was bent. Raymond was met by his manager when he returned to his working station,. Charles Davenport was a graduate of King High School himself and president of the Local School Council.

"Hey! Raymond. Why don't you take the rest of the evening off, we'll be okay." he said, "Yeah man, go home. Get some rest and get-up for the game tomorrow night. Mr. Davenport suggested."

"Hey, thanks Mr. Davenport, that's exactly what I'm going to do. We have a lot to play for tomorrow night." Raymond agreed. "I'm out of here, and thanks again, Mr. Davenport."

Flashing the victory sign, Mr. Davenport shouted, "GET UP ON THE HOOK!" He put two Triple Slap Burgers with bacon, a large order of fries, and a large strawberry shake into a bag and headed to the parking lot where Milton, Eric, and approximately twelve other boys had gathered.

Activities

Understanding what you have read.
Do not write in this book. Use your Raymond Tinsley journal.

PART I: <u>True/False</u>
1. Raymond counted ten cars in the drive-through line.
2. Three girls from Carver were next in line.
3. Police arrested the girls after the fight.
4. The manager told Raymond he could leave early, providing he cleaned up his working area.
5. Raymond and the manager pulled the three girls from Carver off the two girls from Martin Luther King.

PART II: *Fill in the blanks*
Fill in each blank with the correct word from the word list below.
1. After practice, Milton gave Raymond a ride to his after school job at
2. _____ was the night manager at Slap Burgers.
3. Charles Davenport was _____ of Martin Luther King's Local School Council.
4. An old man lost his _____ during the fight.
5. Raymond put two triple Slap Burgers with bacon, a large order of fries, and a _____ into a bag and headed toward the parking lot.

Charles Davenport
false teeth
president
Slap Burger
Strawberry Shake

PART III. *Vocabulary*

Use a dictionary to find the definition of the words listed below. Construct a new sentence for each word. Explain how each word was used in Chapter 3.

escorted
garment
hesitated
intimidate
shreds
statue
summoned
unison

PART IV. *__Writing Prompts__*
Write; Describing your personal reaction to each character.

A. The girls wearing Carver High School Sweaters.
B. The cheerleaders from MLK High School.
C. The old man who lost his false teeth during the fight.

PART V.
Answer the following questions.

A. What started the fight?
B. Could the fight have been avoided? How could it have been avoided? (Class discussion)

Chapter Four

He had seen that look before
He knew something was about to go down
Seven young brothers were killed

The HIV virus: 20% increase among high school students

"Hey! Raymond!" Milton hollered out, "Over here." Raymond walked over where the boys were standing and began eating one of the Triple Slap Burgers.

"It's going on R.T." Eric said walking toward Raymond and extending his right hand forward for the brothers' handshake.

"I hear you, my man. This time tomorrow, we will be four hours away from tip-off," Raymond answered while taking a huge bite from the Triple Slap Burger in his left hand and going through the brothers' shake with his right. He had set the bag with the second burger, large fries, and shake on the hood of Milton's car. Raymond paused for a moment. He looked at the solemn faces of his friends standing around the car. He had seen that look before. He knew something was about to go down. A classmate was killed last year in a drive-by shooting while sitting in a car with his girl. His death ignited a gang war between the schools.

He thought about many of his friends who had been killed or wounded in gang wars. Four of his friends from elementary school had been killed, wounded or paralyzed by drive-by shootings. During his freshman year, one of his team-mates was wounded in a gang war and now needed medical treatments for the rest of his life. He now leads a crusade, from a wheelchair, talking to gang bangers against teen violence.

Seven young brothers were killed between the two gang factions. Flash backs of a rival gang coming to the church where services were being held for one of the slain members and shooting into the casket. These revenge shootings lasted seven months until a mini-truce was agreed upon. Things had quieted down relatively since the truce, but a tiny spark could start another war.

The captured suspects did not attend Carver High School. The one that's on the run is one of Carver's former students. No students currently attending Carver were involved with the King shooting. Raymond took the last bite of the Slap Burger while reaching into the bag and taking out the strawberry shake.

"What's going down?" Raymond asked as he slowly sucked on the strawberry shake from the container through the red and white straw. All the boys came closer to the hood of the car. In a shallow whisper, Eric stepped forward and said, "Some of the brothers are planning a thing for Carver after the game tomorrow night. Win or lose, there must be a retaliation for Coach Mickey's shooting."

"Hey man, let's not do anything stupid," Raymond answered.

"If we don't, they are going to think we are weak and afraid to defend our home turf." Eric whispered.

"Before we left school, we all agreed to chill out until they arrest this dude, Benny D.," Raymond said.

"Yeah, that's exactly what Benny D. wants us to do. He wants us to go out and start shooting each other up, and start a gang war between Carver and King. We'd lose our momentum for the game." Milton said.

"Uh huh, that's what I think Benny D. had planned." Eric exclaimed.

"And, hey, man, listen up. What would Coach Mickey tell us to do if he was here?" Raymond asked. All the boys paused for a moment. Raymond had said just the right thing to put an end to all their irrational plans.

Coach Mickey had often talked about the role he played during the Civil Rights Movement in the South. "I marched with Dr. Martin Luther King, Jr. in Selma, Alabama. I was in line right behind him," he would say. Afterwards, he would end by telling us, "The struggle isn't over. Non-violence is the key to our long-range success."

"Hey, man, you guys think about it before anything goes down. I'm out of here." said Raymond.

"Hold on," Milton called out to Raymond, "I'll drop you off."

"Okay, I want to get home early to work on my project for Mr. William's class." Raymond answered. The rest of the boys also left giving the victory sign to Raymond, Eric, and Milton as they drove away.

Milton put a compact disk in the player and turned the volume up. There were six twelve-inch speakers in the trunk and two in the overhead interior and front doors.

With the JVC 210 equalizer balancing the sound, it gave you the feeling you had the best seats in the house at a Hip Hop concert.

"Hey! Raymond, wait till I run this at you, my brother. My girl and I finally made it last night." Milton said with a smile on his face from ear to ear.

"You mean... you and, uh, what's her name?" Raymond asked.

"Tonya. Tonya Evans," Milton answered, "the finest thing at King High.

"You are lying, everybody on the team has been trying to get to her, and you scored with Tonya Evans? No way, no way!" said Raymond. "I find that really hard to believe, Milton."

"Would I lie to my best partner?" Milton asked with another convincing smile from ear to ear.

"Alright man, I believe you. I believe you," Raymond said. "But, what did you use?" he asked.

"What do you mean? What did I use?" Milton asked back.

"What kind of condom did you use?" Raymond inquired for the second time.

Milton paused for a moment before answering. He never thought that his best friend would question him about the use of a condom when he had made it with one of the finest girls at King High. "What do you mean 'What kind of condom?'"

"Aw, man, this was unexpected, and I didn't have one with me at the time. And, man, like I said, this was a shock to me that she consented." Milton replied.

"Aw, man, that was really dumb, really dumb. It is obvious that you are not aware of the statistics on how the HIV virus is infecting high school students. There has been a twenty percent increase of the HIV virus among high school students over the past four years, and its growing. It takes several years to find out if you have the virus after having sex with someone who is infected. You could have it right now and not even know it. Say, my brother, get smart. Use your head. That virus is out there, and you don't know who has it." Raymond said turning the sound system off

"It was just an unexpected thing that happened, man." Milton said.

Chapter Four

"Yeah, I know," replied Raymond, "I just want you to be around long enough so that you can watch me play when I make it to the NBA."

"Okay, Father," Milton replied, "I got the message." Both boys seriously and responsibly acknowledged the importance of safe sex or no sex.

Hey Milton! Let's run by Darrell's place. The band is rehearsing for an audition with Sony Records. They want me to sing one of the tunes." Raymond said."

"Hey! That's all right, R.T. Yeah, we'll stop for a minute, I want to get home early to work on my senior project." Milton said.

"Yeah, me to." replied Raymond.

There were a few people standing out front when they arrived at Darrell's house. Milton turned on the alarm system in his car, and the two walked past the people standing in the front yard.

"Hey, Raymond, get up on The Hook," someone hollered out of the crowd. Sitting on the side of the curb was a man Raymond had not seen for a few years. Raymond recognized him because he had been his father's best friend before he passed away. Raymond's real father was killed attempting to rob a liquor store. Mr. Harper was with Raymond's dad a few hours before he was killed. He tried to talk Raymond's father out of robbing the liquor store. After that, Mr. Harper's life had gone downhill. He had become a connoisseur of cheap wine, and anything else that would ease the pain from the death of his best friend.

Hey Raymond! You sure look like your daddy." Mr. Harper mumbled. Raymond walked over to the side of the curb where Mr. Harper was braced against the fire plug.

"Mr. Harper, how are you doing, brother?" Raymond asked.

"Man, you are the spitting image of your old man," Mr. Harper said trying to get up and shake Raymond's hand. After a few more attempts, he decided to remain braced to the fire plug. "Say Raymond, you got a dollar? I wanna buy me a Slap Burger."

"Brother Harper, you are the right man in the right place at the right time. You must be living right," Raymond answered while bending down to shake his hand. "I've got a Triple Slap Burger in the car with everything on it."

"Naw, naw, naw, Raymond, I don't want to t-t-take your burger. I want to buy my own," Mr. Harper said while holding a firm grip on the fire plug to maintain his balance."

Raymond knew exactly why Mr. Harper preferred the dollar: another bottle of wine. His friends were probably waiting for him two blocks away at the corner liquor store to combine their change for another bottle. Raymond gave Mr. Harper two dollars. Before the boys could get down the basement stairs where the band was rehearsing, Mr. Harper had gotten up from the curb and was headed in a slow motion glide toward the corner liquor store.

Darrell had turned the basement into a decent rehearsal room. It had acoustical tile on the wall and ceiling. Heavy acoustical lining around the door kept the sound from traveling too far into the community.

The group consisted of drums, keyboards, bass, two guitars, trumpet, two saxophones, and vocalists. Raymond sang with the group on special gigs during the prom season.

"My man, Raymond; my man, Milton," Darrell said, as the two boys entered the basement. Raymond and Darrell went through the brothers' handshake. "Hey man, it's confirmed. Sony Records has offered us a recording contract. Are you coming with the band?" Darrell asked.

"Are you serious?" Raymond asked.

"Man, would I lie to a brother about to get up on The Hook?"

"Am I interested? Man, I would sabotage this band before I let you guys leave town without me!" Raymond answered. The two had a good laugh and went through the brothers' handshake again. Raymond rehearsed three songs with the band. People standing in the front yard when they arrived were now trying to get into the basement to see and hear Raymond sing. "Hey man, we gotta get up. Raymond said handing the microphone to Darrell.

"Hey, I can understand it, brother. I will catch up with you after the game tomorrow night. And hey! get up on The Hook!" Darrell said.

Raymond and Milton left the rehearsal and headed for home. Driving through the hood reminded Raymond of how blessed he was. He had not gotten into any serious trouble, and, thanks to his status as a star basketball player and his determination to make something of himself, he had managed to stay away from drugs and gangbanging.

Activities

Understanding what you have read.
Do not write in this book. *Use your Raymond Tinsley journal*

PART I: <u>True/False</u>
1. Raymond ate the two Slap Burgers while talking to his friends in the parking lot.
2. The boys were planning a thing for Carver after the game.
3. They knew Coach Mickey would approve of their getting revenge.
4. Coach Mickey was third in line behind Dr. King during the march in Selma, Alabama.
5. The sound system in Milton's car gave you the feeling one was at a Hip Hop concert.
6. Raymond told Milton there was an increase in the HIV virus among high school students.
7. Raymond's real father was wounded during a liquor store robbery.
8. Mr. Harper was the pastor of the church Raymond attended.
9. RCA Records had offered the band a recording contract.
10. Raymond was a backup dancer with the band.

PART I Know Your Characters
Match the description with the character.

1. The Musician   A. Mr. Harper
2. The connoisseur of cheap wine   B. Benny D.
3. The person wanted by the police   C. Darrell

PART III Vocabulary
Use a dictionary to find the definition of the words listed below. Construct a new sentence for each word. Explain how each word was used in Chapter 4.

audition	acoustical
irrational	braced
momentum	condom
paused	confirmed
relatively	connoisseur
retaliation	consented
revenge	convincing
rival	equalizer
sabotage	infected
shallow	virus

PART IV *Writing Prompts*
A. Describe your personal reaction to each character.
   1. Darrell
   2. Mr. Harper
B. Write a short skit characterizing the conversation between Raymond and Mister Harper.

WRITING TIPS

Introduction...
TYPES OF WRITING

tells what the story is about. Catches the reader's interest with an unusual:description, and opening questions, an interesting fact, or a humorous statement.

Body

supports your introduction by providing details and examples to develop the ideas you said you would talk about in the introduction.

Conclusion...

ties everything together. This is the ending of your story and should be as important, clear and interesting as your introduction. It is the last impression the reader has about the story

Narration

Intent:
> tell a story
> recount a personal experience
> report an observed event

Exposition

Intent:
Inform
Explain

Persuasion

Intent
Convince
Influence
Motivate

Description

Intent:
Appeal to the senses
Create a mood

Creative Expression

Intent:
Relate imaginative or factual experiences and ideas.
Express thoughts and feeling

UNIT I TEST
Chapters 1-4

Name _____ Score _____

PART I. True/False (60 points)
1. Senior projects were due the first week in June.
2. Clarence Johnson was known for his jump shot.
3. The Hook had to be stopped if there was any chance of their winning the Championship game.
4. The coach told Raymond he had to develop his own strategy on how the Hook should be guarded.
5. The speeding car with automatic assault weapons was headed south on 79 Street.
6. "Down, Coach!" Milton screamed out when the shooting started.
7. Raymond took cover behind the bronze statue of Martin Luther King.
8. Eric cried out, "I've been hit."
9. Milton went for help.
10. Raymond was out in the street to direct the first paramedics.
11. The office's secretary told Milton she had already called for help.
12. Coach Mickey had been wounded twice.
13. They immediately rushed Coach Mickey to Somerest Memorial Hospital.
14. Raymond and Eric rode in the ambulance with the coach.
15. Coach Mickey told Raymond he would be out of the hospital in time to coach the game.
16. The police had arrested three suspects and had a strong lead on the fourth shooter.
17. Benny D. was a member of the Carver High Basketball Team.
18. Coach Mickey told Raymond he should develop a game plan for the Championship game.
19. Raymond counted ten cars in the drive-through line.
20. Three girls from Carver were next in line.
21. Police arrested the girls after the fight.
22. The manager told Raymond he could leave early, providing he cleaned up his work area.
23. Raymond and the manager pulled the three girls from Carver off the two girls from Martin Luther King.
24. Raymond ate the two Slap Burgers while talking to his friends in the parking Lot.
25. The boys were planning a thing for Carver after the game.
26. They knew Coach Mickey would approve of their getting revenge.
27. Coach Mickey was third in line behind Dr. King during the march in Selma, Alabama.
28. The sound system in Milton's car gave the feeling one was at a live Hip Hop concert.
29. Raymond told Milton there was an increase in the HIV virus among high school students.
30. Raymond's real father was wounded during a liquor store robbery.

PART II *Know Your Characters* (20 points)

1. The boy rapping to the girl in the hall.
2. The teammate who helped Raymond escort Milton to the gym
3. The 6'9" senior basketball star for MartinLuther King High School
4. The basketball coach.
5. The 7' 1" senior basketball star for Carver HighSchool.
6. The teacher.
7. The musician.
8. The connoisseur of wine.
9. The person wanted by the police.
10. Raymond's best friend

A. Raymond
B. Clarence.
C. Mickey
D. Mr. Williams
E. Eric
F. Milton
G. Mr. Harper
H. Benny D.
I. Darrell
J. Mr. Davenport

PART III Fill in the blanks (10 points)
1. After practice, Milton gave Raymond a ride to his after school job at_____
2. _____ was the night manager at Slap Burgers.
3. Charles Davenport was President of Martin Luther King's_____
4. An old man lost his _____ during the fight.
5. Raymond put two double Slap Burgers with cheese, a large order of fries, and a _____ into a bag and headed toward the parking lot.

false teeth
Local School Council
Slap Burgers
strawberry shake
Mr. Davenport

PART IV *Writing Prompts* (10 points)
1. Describe the fight between the girls from MLK and Carver. Be sure to include the answers to the following questions.
    A. What started the fight? How could it have been avoided?

Chapter Five

Evelyn (Dee Dee) a crack user
Her friend Latisha
We're just hanging out trying to make something happen

Milton finds the kids in the bedroom playing with a cigarette lighter

Raymond asked Milton to pull over when they reached the corner of 117th and Jackson, "What's up, R.T., I don't like stopping over here. Don't you remember last year Jamal was killed right here in a drive-by" said Milton.

Raymond got out of the car and walked back to where two women were standing in an alley between two condemned buildings.

"Hey, R.T., those are just some petty prostitutes. What's wrong with you man? Let's get out of here," Milton exclaimed.

Raymond continued walking toward the women while calling one of them by name. "Evelyn, Evelyn Williams," Raymond called out to one of the women.

"Hey girl, what's up? What are you doing down here? I thought you lived with your mother over on Lockwood."

Slowly turning to Raymond's voice, she muttered, "Aw, hey, hey, Raymond, this is my friend, Latisha. We're just hanging out trying to make something happen."

Before Raymond's older brother joined the Marines, he and Evelyn had a child --Curtis Jr. Evelyn was a crack user and worked as a petty prostitute to support her habit. Raymond had not seen Evelyn Dee Dee since his sophomore year at MLK High.

"I got my own place now. Mamma and I couldn't get along," she said.

"Hey y-y, that's good. How is little Curtis junior and your baby? I like to see them." Raymond asked.

"Aw! Raymond! Not you too! It's like I told that dumb #$#$!#@!!! Case worker from DCFS; (Department of Children and Family Services), my kids can take care of themselves. Curtis Jr. knows how to fix his own breakfast, and he is learning how to fix stuff on the stove. I never leave them alone no more than an hour," she angrily answered.

Milton and Raymond looked at each other in disgust knowing that Dee Dee had a very serious drug problem if she allowed a four-year-old kid to use a gas stove. Dee Dee was so involved with drugs that she never thought about the health hazards and deaths of young children left at home alone unsupervised. Raymond knew he had to find out more about Dee Dee's life style and the condition of Curtis Jr. and the baby.

"Where do you live Dee Dee? I really want to see Curtis Jr. and the baby," Raymond demanded.

"I live around the corner, third building on the left, 116 West Jackson. You are even worse than that ##**## caseworker from DCFS (Department of Children and Family Services). I don't know why you are asking all these ##**## questions about me and my kids. I told your ##**#%# mother that we are doing just fine," she answered angrily in a high pitched voice.

"With you or without you Dee Dee, I am going to see Curtis Jr. before I leave," Raymond said.

Raymond and Milton began walking in the direction of the apartment building. Walking slowly behind them, Evelyn continued cursing Raymond.

"I am not ready to go home now. Latisha and I are waiting for a package from a friend. He should be here anytime now," she answered.

"Aw, come on Dee Dee," I just want to see him for a minute. You and your friend Latisha can get back together when I leave," Raymond replied.

Lighting a joint, Latisha turned to Dee Dee. "This is Curtis junior's uncle. I'll be here when you get back, and I'll hold on to the package when Gary shows up. Okay?"

"Okay, Okay!" Dee Dee shouted, "Let's go see Curtis Jr.

"Tisha, don't you get rid of that package before I get back," she demanded.

Milton set the burglar alarm on the car and the three walked around the corner to Dee Dee's apartment building. Two dudes were smoking marijuana in the hallway when they arrived. Another dude, sitting on the third step with a cellophane bag containing two syringes was screaming every five or more seconds.

"Ain't you R.T.? Don't you play ball for Martin Luther King?" one of the boys smoking marijuana asked.

"Yeah, yeah," Raymond answered, but continued walking toward the staircase. People were looking out their doors to see who was coming up the stairs. The building housed mostly single parent families with one to four kids.

The door was open when they reached Evelyn's apartment. Shouting in a high pitched voice, she began calling out to Curtis Jr. "Curtis Jr.! Curtis Jr.! Where are you? You little ##**##!." she shouted.

"In here," Milton called back to them. Milton had gone into the bedroom where he found Curtis Jr., the baby who was one year old, and a three year old boy from a neighboring apartment playing with a cigarette lighter near the window. Evelyn went through her thing with Curtis Jr. about playing with fire, and told the visiting boy to go home.

Evelyn sat on the side of the bed holding the baby with Curtis Jr. by her side and began crying. Raymond and Milton stood there for a moment and watched Evelyn and her two kids cry. Evelyn realized that this situation could have turned out differently if Raymond and Milton had not insisted on seeing Curtis Jr. Without saying anything, Raymond and Milton walked out the door and back to the car.

Activities

Understanding what you have read.
Do not write in this book Use your Raymond Tinsley journal.

PART I: True/False
1. Raymond asked Milton to stop at the McDonald's on Jackson.
2. Dee Dee was a junior at Carver High School.
3. Dee Dee and Latisha were standing between two condemned buildings.
4. Dee Dee's mother kept the three boys for her when she was working.
5. Raymond had not seen Dee Dee since his sophomore year at MLK.
6. Dee Dee took good care of her kids.
7. She never left them alone.
8. Curtis Junior knew not to ever play with cigarette lighters and matches.
9. After talking with Dee Dee at McDonald's, Raymond and Milton headed home.
10. The man with the syringes appeared to be a normal person.
11. Latisha told Evelyn that Raymond should stay out of her business.
12. The Department of Children and Family Services told Evelyn she was doing a good job raising her kids.
13. When they reached the apartment, Curtis Jr. greeted them at the door.
14. After they discovered the kids in the living room, Dee Dee told Raymond and Milton to leave.

Discuss 4, 5, 8, 9, 10, and 12

PART II Completions
Fill in each blank with the correct word from the word list.
1. Dee Dee had _____ kids.
2. Dee Dee and Latisha were waiting for a package from _____
3. _____ was four years old.
4. The kids were playing with a _____ near the curtains in the bedroom.
5. Evelyn sat on the side of the bed and _____ after she realized the situation in which she had placed her kids.

cigarette lighter
Curtis Junior
Gary
cried
dangerous
two

PART III Vocabulary
Use a dictionary to find the definition for the words listed below. Construct a new sentence for each word Explain how each word was used in Chapter 5.

angrily	hazards
prostituted	condemned
high pitched	situation
dangerous	insisted
syringe	demanded
muttering	unsupervised

PART IV: *Questions to Discuss*
A. Discuss why kids should not be left unsupervised.
B. Do you think Dee Dee will leave her kids alone again? Explain your answer.
C. If you had the resources, and money, how would you help adolescents like Dee Dee?
D. At age 17, with two kids, is it too late for Dee Dee to turn her life around?
E. Approximately how old was Dee Dee when she had her first child?

PART V. *Writing Prompts*
Write your personal reactions to Dee Dee, Latisha, and the person sitting on the steps with a cellophane bag containing two syringes and screaming every five or more seconds.

Chapter Six

An attempt to destroy the game plan
The criminally insane drug dealer

Benny D., wanted by the police

An ambulance and police car were parked in front of the house when they returned to the two-flat where Raymond lived. Raymond's Aunt Jean met them at the door. She explained what was going on. She told Raymond that his stepfather had been mugged by two boys. "He's okay, but he refuses to go for a checkup. He wants no part of the hospital. Please try and convince him to go," she said. Raymond walked into the room where the paramedics and police were questioning his stepfather.

"I'm okay, son, those dudes didn't really get to your old man. I flattened the big guy. The other one ran. The little dude hit me from behind. I bumped my head on the pavement during the fall. But I'm okay. You see, they didn't expect me to get up after the little dude hit me from behind, but I managed to get up and keep my composure. I know I landed three good punches out of the seven or eight I threw. I knew the big boy was hurting because he also turned and ran in the same direction as the little guy, and I almost caught up with him before he turned the corner," he said.

"I know, Dad. I'm sure you're okay, but it wouldn't hurt to have a checkup at the hospital," Raymond said. His stepfather pretended not to hear a word Raymond had said. As he was escorting the policemen and paramedics out of the room, Raymond demanded the policemen nail his stepfather's assailants. "The big one is probably somewhere trying to get medical attention, too," said Raymond. "You have a tough old man," whispered a policeman as he walked out the door.

Gerald, Raymond's youngest brother, was also in the bedroom. "It was some dudes from Carver," he said. "What!" exclaimed Raymond. "I'll kill 'em! I'll kill 'em!"

Milton walked into the room trying to hold back his tears and anger about the whole situation. "We'll get 'em. We'll get 'em, Raymond," replied Milton. "One of them goes by the name of Benny D.," said Gerald. "What!" said Raymond and Milton. "That's the same dude who is suspected of shooting up our campus today. He is probably the same guy who shot Coach Mickey!" yelled Raymond.

Raymond lifted his right hand above his head and said, "I'm gonna kill them dirty ###***!!I ***##

"Hey, hey, hey!" yelled Raymond's stepfather. "I know how you guys feel. You're angry, mad, and hurt; but you see, this is all part of his plan to upset you emotionally and throw you off your game plan."

"Yeah, Raymond, this is what Coach Mickey was saying in the hospital," said Milton. The stepfather intervened, "You guys don't need to get involved with this mess, especially right now with the big game tomorrow. Let the police handle it. They know exactly who these guys are."

"I hope they do that, Dad, because I have friends that would love to find Benny D. before the cops do. Some dudes from the south side are also looking for him. The word out on the streets is that

Benny D. and three other dudes robbed two crack houses last night. And man, you know these people don't play fair when it comes to drugs," said Gerald.

"Benny D. is a cocaine-, crack-head, criminally insane man who is extremely dangerous, "said the stepfather.

After Milton left, Raymond, Gerald, and his stepfather stayed up late talking about Benny D. and the shootings of the students and Coach Mickey at school. The drive-by was the top news story on all the late-night, local networks. Each station repeatedly flashed police mug shots of Benny D. and others wanted for a variety of crimes.

After the news, Raymond worked on his senior project. His last thought before falling asleep was Coach Mickey's coaching him to Get Up On The Hook

Activities

Understanding what you have read.
Do not write in this book Use your Raymond Tinsley journal.

PART I True/False
1. Raymond's stepfather was unable to get out of bed.
2. It was suspected that four boys from MLK mugged Raymond's stepfather.
3. It was believed that Benny D. was a cocaine, crack-head, criminally insane person.
4. After the ten o'clock news, Raymond fell asleep on the couch.
5. The last thought before falling asleep was how to smoke out Benny D. Discuss 3

PART II: Completions
Fill in each blank with the correct word from the word list.
1. An _____ and a _____ car were parked in front of the house when they arrived.
2. _____ met them at the door.
3. Raymond's stepfather had been mugged by _____ boys.
4. You got a tough old man, whispered one of the _____
5. Raymond's last thought before falling asleep was _____

ambulance
Aunt Jean
getting up on The Hook
police car
policemen
two

PART III Vocabulary
Use a dictionary to find the definition of the words listed below. Construct a new sentence for each word Explain how each word was used in Chapter 6.

anger
assailants
composure
criminally insane
exclaimed
flashed intervened mugged
repeatedly
routine
variety

27

PART IV. Writing Prompts
In Chapter 6, Raymond discovers the boys involved in the drive-by shooting are the same boys suspected of mugging his stepfather. What would your reaction be if you were Raymond? (Write and discuss)

Chapter Seven

The morning workout
A mother's wish
The jamming Pep rally
Two funky tunes by the MLK band

The red plastic covering the exit sign shatters and falls to the floor

Raymond was up early the next morning. He ate a bowl of raisin bran and grabbed two oranges from fruit bowl on the dining room table before heading for the park for his morning workout.

He began his morning workout after joining up with his friends at the park. He stretched his fast paced run from three to four miles trying to forget what had happened yesterday. He knew that this attack was some type of ploy to throw him off his game plan. There were a lot of questions that had to be answered he thought. If this is true, Raymond thought, I really need to get up on The Hook.

Raymond returned home after his morning workout. He waited for his mother on the front steps of the house. His mother worked the night shift at Somerset Memorial Hospital and would be on her way home. Raymond went out to the street to greet his mother when she arrived. He picked her up and carried her to the front porch. "Put me down, Raymond Tinsley!" shrieked his mother lovingly. "You are just like your father."

They sat on the front porch and talked about the team, his grades in school and the possibilities of attending college in the fall. "The shootings were on the news, Raymond. I am so afraid each time you leave in the morning for school," she said somberly. Raymond responded, "I know Mom but I don't have but two more months of school. My grades are up and the only big requirement before graduation is the senior project for my English IV class. Other than that, I will graduate."

"You have a big game tonight, Right?" she asked. "Yeah, that's right Mom. I wish you could be there to see me go up on The Hook. It's just another game. The only difference is the intensity," Raymond replied.

With tears in her eyes, she turned to Raymond and said, "Just be careful. I want you to go as far as you can with your education and basketball." "Mom, don't worry. I'll be fine, you'll see," Raymond said to console her.

Raymond took a quick shower and dressed for school. Milton was coming by to pick him up. Milton honked the car horn when he arrived. "Hey Mom, I gotta run. We have a team meeting with the principal this morning at 8 o'clock," said Raymond. At the meeting, the principal reminded the team of the noontime pep rally in the gymnasium. The team left the meeting and headed for their first period class.

At 11:30, the students began assembling in the gymnasium. The King High School band opened the assembly with two funky selections featuring the percussion section. The entire student body and staff got involved. "Get up on The Hook, get up on The Hook," shouted the students as the team came out and took their places on the stage. The principal introduced the team and handed the microphone to Raymond.

"R.T., R.T, R.T.," chanted the student body. The noise was so loud it shattered the red plastic cover over the exit sign at the rear of the gymnasium. After seven minutes of cheering and yelling, the students quieted so that Raymond could make his short speech. He walked slowly to the front of the stage and started to rap:

> I know you are wondering what's really going down
> It's no longer a secret; it's all about the clown
> We will meet tonight in the downtown gym
> And you better believe I'm going up on him
> They tried to intimidate me, even beat up my old man
> But he's going doing okay, this strengthened my game plan
> I work out everyday and read good books
> So come out tonight and watch me "Get up On the Hook"

Everybody was up on their feet cheering after Raymond's rapping speech. Teachers and students were dancing in the aisles. The percussion pumped up the audience with its accompaniment to the shouts of 'Get up on the Hook, Get up on the Hook'. The principal and the librarian waltzed together on stage. After the speech, Raymond knew that he had achieved the mental plateau and peak preparedness for the championship game. The students and staff joined right hand over left hand and sang the school anthem.

Activities

Understanding what you have read.
Do not write in this book Use your Raymond Tinsley journal

PART I: True/False
1. Raymond overslept the next morning?
2. He stretched his fast paced run from three to four miles trying to forget what had happened yesterday.
3. Raymond waited for his mother at the bus stop.
4. Raymond's mother worked the night shift at Somerest Memorial Hospital.
5. Raymond and his mother talked about the team, his grades, and the possibility of his going to college.
6. Raymond told his mother his grades were down, and he may have to attend summer school.
7. The big requirement before graduation was his senior project for Mr. William's English IV class.
8. At the meeting, the principal reminded the team of the noon pep rally in the auditorium.
9. MLK band opened the pep rally with two selections: Stars and Stripes Forever and the Theme From Madame Butterfly.
10. In his rap to the student body, Raymond explained what had happened and how he planned to 'go up' on The Hook.
11. Everybody was up on their feet after Raymond's speech.
12. Teachers and students began fighting in the aisles.
13. The principal and the librarian jumped off the stage.
14. The trumpet section would accent with the audience each time they yelled 'Get up on The Hook.'
15. The noise was so intense that the red plastic covering the exit sign shattered into little pieces and fell to the floor.

Discuss #5-7

PART II Vocabulary
Use a dictionary to find the definition of the words listed below. Construct a new sentence for each word. Explain how each word was used in Chapter 7.

accompaniment
anthem
chanted
console
gymnasium
intensity

intimidate
librarian
lovingly
pace
percussion
ploy
preparedness
requirement
respond
shrieked
strengthened
waltzed

PART III: Writing Prompts
A. Write, describing the conversation between Raymond and his mother.
B. In rap style, dramatize Raymond's speech to the student body.

<u>Practice the rap with the CD Sound Track included with this book</u>
(See Enclosure)

Chapter Eight

Jesse Owens Park
Cassandra Hawkins, fine and smart
NBA dreams
The new frontier

The judicial system

After the assembly, Raymond asked the members of the team to return to school at 6:00.

"Hey, Raymond! What do you wanna do?" asked Milton. "I don't know. It might be nice to go down to the park and just chill out before the game," Raymond replied.

The boys left the school and headed for nearby Jesse Owens Park. The park was a memorial to famous past and present black American athletes. A large display room of Jesse Owens contributions to sports was exhibited on the park grounds. Trophies, pictures, videos and film shots of the eight gold medals he won in the 1941 Olympics held in Germany were displayed for all to see and admire.

The two boys talked basketball all the way to the park. Raymond, up for the championship game, changed his sneakers and headed for the open space. "Hey, Raymond! Wait up for me, dude!" shouted Milton. Milton sprinted to catch up with his pal who was at the far end of the park. "How many do you want to do?" asked Milton. "I don't know. Three or four. I just want to release some of this energy," Raymond said as he picked up the pace leaving Milton behind.

The boys ran five fast laps, about two and half miles, around the park. After the workout, the boys walked across the street to the 7-11 store for something to eat and drink. They were greeted by a sweet, soft voice. "Hi, Raymond."

The voice belonged to Cassandra Hawkins. She was at the convenience store gas pump with her father who was buying gas for their car.

Before Raymond could recognize the voice, Cassandra was out of the car and walking towards him. Cassandra was a fine sister. Raymond met Cassandra at the Regional Three Track Meet last year. Ever since then, they talked to each other by phone but had not yet dated.

She was appealing in her designer jeans and Blue-Blocker sun shades. According to Raymond, not only was she fine, but she was smart as well. Cassandra was a senior at the Malcolm X High School.

She ranked number three in her senior class of one hundred and seventy-six students. Her overall grade point average was 3.9. She was a track runner, captain of the varsity girl's volleyball team and recipient of many academic and athletic plaques and trophies. She, too, had applied to, and was accepted by, a number of colleges and universities across the country. She had decided to attend Pepperdine University in Southern Cal4fornia in the fall and pursue a biology major. She planned to become a physician.

He greeted her with a kiss on her cheek as her father looked on from the gas pump. "Oh, Raymond, I want you to meet my father," said Cassandra. "Dad, this is Raymond Tinsley and his friend and team member, Milton Jones."

"Nice meeting you brothers. I wish you luck in tonight's game," said Mr. Hawkins.

"Nice meeting you too, sir," answered Milton. Mr. Hawkins addressed his daughter, "Cassandra, pay for the gas and bring me a large Slurpy."

"Okay, Dad."

Inside the store, the three walked back to the beverage cooler. "What's up R.T.? I haven't heard from you in about a month," said Cassandra. "I know, I know. I planned to call you this week but you know that so much has gone down recently and...."

"I know too," interrupted Cassandra. "I have been watching it on television."

Milton, trying to remember where he had met her, stood by listening to Raymond. Then it hit him. "Now I remember!" exclaimed Milton. "You won the 440 last year at the Regional Three Track Meet. Yeah, yeah, that's where I remember seeing you. . . at Regional Three!"

"Hey, that's right," Cassandra replied.

"fine as you are, Milton said, "how can anyone forget?"

Raymond saw the conversation going into another direction. Raymond knew that it would become a one-sided conversation if he allowed Milton to continue talking. O-P-P, 0-P-P Chill out homie, "Raymond said to Milton."

"Take care," Cassandra said as she began walking backwards towards her car.

"I'll call you this week," Raymond said as he noticed a man checking Cassandra out as she walked to the car in her tight skinny jeans. "Cassandra could cause a accident wearing the outfit she has on," Raymond thought to himself.

A man in a car with his wife, looking in his rearview mirror ran into the side of the building and damaged the Pepsi machine trying to get a good look at Cassandra. His wife was beating him with her purse because he was not paying attention to his driving.

The boys bought some drinks and returned to the park. Raymond found a shady spot near the duck pond to rest. Milton went through a series of sit-up exercises nearby. "UCLA, here I come," Raymond shouted. "UCLA is a big school, so big that it will take a year for you to find your way around the place. They have eight or more schools on the same campus," Milton said.

"Yeah," said Raymond.

"So, what do you want to major in?" asked Milton.

"I'm not sure yet. I'm interested in space exploration and want to take some courses in the space studies program at UCLA. Outer space is the new frontier, and I want to be a pioneer in space exploration. Do you realize that space scientists are collecting data now that estimates the age of the universe?

"You know, it reminds me of the early West, when men tried to settle there. I can see myself talking to and meeting inhabitants of other planets. Don't you remember Mr. Bates talking about the Big Bang theory in our Physics class? He said that one of the theories of how the universe came to be was from a gigantic explosion of mass. With the help of the Hubble telescope, space scientists are getting data that estimates the age of the universe. Ripples from the explosion created the universe. The planets, stars, moon

Chapter Eight

and sun are ripples from that gigantic explosion. So if there is life on earth, there must be other forms of life out there in the universe."

"Hey, man," interrupted Milton. "You are really getting into this space thing. I have been thinking seriously about majoring in law. Have you read the statistics on young black American males? I saw the numbers of brothers between the ages of eighteen and twenty-six who are in prison. It really got to me.".

"Hey man, you just talked to me about my space thing and now here you are talking about law. You think you got it together, huh dude?" asked Raymond. "What role do you want to play in law, I mean... what are your goals... .do you want to become a judge, Milton?" Raymond continued. "How will you help our brothers, young males our age?"

"You want to be a judge or a lawyer or something?" asked Raymond to his friend.

"Both," replied Milton.

"I thought you would never ask. I am not trying to be God, but a large percent of brothers in jail could have been productive citizens f they had been fairly taken through the judicial system. I am talking about those brothers who had a choice to go either way. Some of them made bad choices in life. I just feel that I could make a difference if I knew more about how the judicial system was set up. I would like to expand the justice system for guys our age so that they are getting a fair deal"

"Man, I can see you in the courtroom sitting on the bench with the bailiff saying, 'the court's in session, the Honorable Judge Milton Jones presiding," responded Raymond. The boys supported each other's dream with a brothers' handshake.

Time went by fast as the two friends talked about college life. "Hey Milton, it's almost five o'clock. I want to go by the house before returning to school," Raymond said.

Activities

Understanding what you have read.
Do not write in this book Use your Raymond Tinsley journal.

PART I. True/False
1. In Raymond's physics class, Mr. Bates explained the theory of the Big Bang.
2. Milton felt that a larger percentage of brothers in jail could have been productive citizens if they had been fairly taken through the judicial system.
3. Milton wanted to become a lawyer and a judge.
4. Milton expressed no concern over the number of young black men in prisons.
5. The boys talked about college life until the first light of day.

PART II: Completions
Fill in each blank with the correct word from the word list.
1. After the assembly, Raymond asked the team to return to school at ____ p.m.
2. Raymond stated he was going down to the park and just _____ out.
3. The boys left school and headed for _____ park.
4. A large display room of _____ contributions to sports was exhibited on the park grounds.
5. After the workout, the boys walked across the street to _____
6. Raymond met Cassandra Hawkins at the _____ track meet last year.
7. Cassandra attended _____ High School.
8. Raymond said he had a great interest in the _____ programs.
9. Milton said he plans to major in _____
10. Raymond met Cassandra at the _____ track meet.

chill out
Regional Ill
Jesse Owens
Seven-Eleven
law
6:00p.m.
Malcolm X
space exploration

36

UNIT II TEST
Chapters 5-8

Name _____ Score _____ Homeroom _____

PART I. True/False (90 points)

_____ 1. Raymond asked Milton to stop at the McDonald's on Jackson.
_____ 2. Dee Dee was a junior at Carver High School.
_____ 3. Dee Dee and Latisha were standing between two condemned buildings.
_____ 4. Dee Dee's mother kept the three boys for her when she was working.
_____ 5. Raymond had not seen Dee Dee since his sophomore year at MLK..
_____ 6. Dee Dee took good care of her kids.
_____ 7. She never left them alone.
_____ 8. Curtis Junior knew not to ever play with cigarette lighters and matches.
_____ 9. After talking with Dee Dee at McDonald's, Raymond and Milton headed home.
_____ 10. The man with the syringes appeared to be a normal person.
_____ 11. Latisha told Evelyn that Raymond should stay out of her business.
_____ 12. The Department of Children and Family Services told Evelyn she was doing a good job raising her kids.
_____ 13. She never left the kids unattended.
_____ 14. When they reached the apartment, Curtis Junior greeted them at the door.
_____ 15. After they discovered the kids in the living room, Dee Dee told Raymond and Milton to leave.
_____ 16. Raymond's stepfather was unable to get out of bed.
_____ 17. Raymond told Milton there was an increase in the HIV virus among high school students.
_____ 18. Raymond's real father was wounded during a liquor store robbery.
_____ 19. Mr. Harper was the pastor of the church Raymond attended.
_____ 20. RCA Records had offered the band a recording contract.
_____ 21. Raymond was a backup dancer for the band.
_____ 22. Raymond overslept the next morning.
_____ 23. He stretched his fast pace run from three to four miles trying to forget what happen on yesterday.
_____ 24. Raymond waited for his mother at the bus stop.
_____ 25. Raymond's mother worked the night shift at Somerest Memorial Hospital.
_____ 26. Raymond and his mother talked about the team, his grades, and the possibility of his going to college.
_____ 27. Raymond told his mother his grades were down and that he might have to attend summer school
_____ 28. The big requirement before graduation was his senior project for Mr. William's English IV class.
_____ 29. At the meeting, the principal reminded the team of the noon pep rally in the auditorium.
_____ 30. The MLK band opened the pep rally with two selections: The Stars and Stripes Forever and the theme from Madame Butterfly.

_____ 31. In his rap to the student body, Raymond explained what had happened and how he planned to 'up on the Hook.
_____ 32. Everyone was up on their feet after Raymond's speech.
_____ 33. Teachers and students began fighting in the aisles.
_____ 34. The principal and the librarian jumped off the stage.
_____ 35. The trumpet section would accent with the audience each time they yelled 'Get up on The Hook.'
_____ 36. The noise was so intense that the red plastic covering the exit sign shattered into little pieces and fell to the floor.
_____ 37. In Raymond's physics class, Mr. Bates explained the theory of the Big Bang.
_____ 38. Milton felt that a larger percent of brothers in jail could have been productive citizens if they had been fairly taken through the judicial system.
_____ 39. Milton wanted to become a lawyer and a judge.
_____ 40. Milton expressed no concern over the number of young black men in prison.
_____ 41. The boys talked about college life until the first light of day.
_____ 42. Milton felt that a larger percent of brothers in jail could have been productive citizens if they had been fairly taken through the judicial system.
_____ 43. Milton wanted to become a lawyer and a judge.
_____ 44. Milton expressed no concern over the number of young black men in prisons.
_____ 45. The boys talked about college life until the first light of day.

PART II. Writing Prompts (10 points)
In Chapter 5, Dee Dee and Latisha were waiting for a package from Gary. Explain what you think the package contained. Defend your answer.

Chapter Nine

This smoke will have you jumping over The Hook
The Eddie Murphy and Martin Lawrence Show
A case of amnesia
The big surprise

The winning lottery ticket

The boys left the park feeling confident they were up for tonights Championship game. Milton dropped Raymond off at home and promised to return at 5:45 a.m.

Gerald, Raymond's youngest brother and some friends were sitting on the front porch smoking marijuana when he arrived. They were talking about Benny D. and the boys that mugged his stepfather.

One of the boys offered Raymond marijuana. "Hey, Raymond," he shouted, "come on, hit the joint Two hits of this will get you up for the game. This smoke will have you doing things you have never done before. You talk about going up on The Hook; this smoke will have you jumping over The Hook." Gerald and his friends laughed about Raymond jumping over The Hook.

"I can see Raymond's Air-Jordan's in The Hook's face when he tries to hook," another boy said laughing so hard tears began rolling down his cheeks.

"Yeah," Raymond answered. Raymond knocked the marijuana out the hand of the boy who was laughing. He pushed him into the hedges adjacent to the house. He grabbed Gerald and pinned him down to the porch. By that time, the three other boys had taken off and were half way down the block. He tightened up on Gerald's shirt and bounced his head several times on the porch. "Gerald, what's wrong with you, man?" Raymond asked.

"Hey, take it easy!" Gerald retorted trying to hold his composure and desperately trying to work his way out of the grip Raymond had on his neck. "My partners were setting something up for the dudes that jumped the old man."

"Are you going out of your mind, Gerald? The only thing you and your partners are going to do is make matters worse. Smoking marijuana only adds to the problem," Raymond continued, "Man, I was confident you would be the man to help Mom and Dad when I go off to college. Man, you got a serious problem when you have to resort to drugs."

Gerald got off the floor and walked to the end of the porch. "I was mad about this Benny D. dude," he said, "We were just trying to find a way to make him pay."

"Yeah, I can understand it." Raymond replied. "But smoking marijuana only seems like a temporary solution to the problem. It really isn't. The police and everyone else know who these guys are. Let the police handle it, Gerald."

"I hear you. I hear you." Gerald answered.

Raymond walked around back to the garage. He found his stepfather leaning over the fence talking to Mr. Duncan. Mr. Duncan had been a good neighbor and friend of Raymond's stepfather for a number of years. He also knew Raymond's real father before he was killed in the attempted liquor store robbery. Mr. Duncan and Raymond's stepfather went to all of the home basketball games. They strongly supported Raymond's quest to go to college.

"Hey, Dad, Mr. Duncan, what's up? Raymond asked. "Whenever you two guys get together, it means something is going down."

"What is wrong with this kid, Brother Duncan?" Raymond's stepfather asked. "Do you think this championship game has gotten to him? He was a normal kid when he left home this morning. You would think that a star basketball player, and future freshman at UCLA could deal with the reality of being a star." Raymond's stepfather said, with an expression of surprise on his face, "I can't believe it." His facial expression changed from surprise to humorous.

"You know, you might be right, Herman," Mr. Duncan answered. "The same thing happened to me when I signed that ten million dollar contract with the Chicago Bears! At that time, we called it a case of amnesia."

"AMNESIA! A case of AMNESIA! Naw man, not Raymond Tinsley, uh uh. I know this kid," Raymond's stepfather said going through a Martin Lawrence stage routine.

"Is that right?" Mr. Duncan asked going through an Eddie Murphy routine.

"Okay, Martin Lawrence. I hear you too, Eddie Murphy," Raymond chuckled. The three had a good laugh about the ten million dollar contract with the Chicago Bears and Raymond's case of amnesia.

The three talked about the championship game with Carver High School. Raymond told them of the plan he and Coach Mickey had put together to guard The Hook. After about ten minutes of basketball talk, Raymond said good night to the two men and began walking towards the house. He saw a car in the garage. He knew neither his mom nor his stepfather owned an automobile. "Hey dad, this car . ... I mean ... who does this car belong to?" Raymond asked with uncontrollable emotions.

"You know what, Raymond Tinsley? You have always managed to be in the right place at the wrong time. Your mother is going to kill me. The car is a graduation gift from the two of us In fact, we had planned to give it to you tonight, after the game, win or lose."

"Are you serious, dad? Is this really my ride?" Raymond asked. "Go in the house and get the keys. They are in the kitchen on top of the refrigerator ."

Raymond was back with the keys before his stepfather could raise the garage door. Raymond couldn't believe this was happening to him. He never thought he would get a car as a graduation gift. Raymond backed the car out of the garage into the alley.

"Nice ride," Gerald said, walking to the front of the car where Raymond's stepfather was standing. Mr. Duncan and Raymond were listening to the purr of the motor. Gerald checked out the sound system.

"Hey, don't get any ideas about driving this car, Raymond," his stepfather said, "if you don't score fifteen points and make ten assists in tonight's championship game, I will be driving this car tomorrow."

"Hey, Dad, I know where you are coming from, but you got to understand. I plan to get up on The Hook."

Chapter Nine

"My man, my man," Mr. Duncan said, "I love to hear you talk like that." He went back into his Eddie Murphy routine chanting, "Get up on The Hook, Raymond, get up on The Hook, get up on The Hook!"

Raymond began talking while getting out of the car and began rubbing the chrome bearing his initials, R.T. , "how did you and Mom, uh, you know, you know what I trying to ask?"

"How could we afford a car like this? Is that what you are thinking?" Raymond's stepfather said as he turned to Mr. Duncan and asked, "Do you think the kid can handle this, Bro Duncan?"

"Give it to him straight," Mr. Duncan answered.

Turning back to Raymond, he said, "Your mother hit the lottery about two months ago. She was one of four winners on a five spot ticket The ticket paid $6,000 to each winner. Your mother paid $3,000 cash for this car."

"WHAT!" Raymond jumped straight up in the air giving high fives to all three. He jumped over the small fence in the back yard and ran four laps shouting, "All right! All right! All right!"

Turning to Mr. Duncan, Raymond's stepfather said, "Let's go stop this kid before he kills himself."

"Hey, Raymond!" they called out to him in unison, "it's just a car."

"I know, I know! This is very uplifting to me and I can't contain how I feel," Raymond called back. "Man, you and Mom are too much!"

"Hold on Raymond, you didn't let me fmish, your mother is saving the rest of the money for your college education, just in case you don't get a scholarship." he said. "O yeah, she is taking off work tonight to come see you play."

"All right, Dad," Raymond said, "I don't want to spoil the surprise." Taking a last glimpse at the car, Raymond slowly backed away from the garage and walked to the front of the house. He and Gerald sat on the front porch and continued their talk about Benny D.

"It's twenty minutes to six," Raymond said, "Milton should be driving up soon." Before Gerald could answer, Milton pulled up in front of the house and honked his horn.

"Let's make it." Milton called out. The two boys left for Martin Luther King High School feeling confident they would win the championship game."

Activities

Understanding what you have read.
Do not write in this book Use your Raymond Tinsley journal.

PART I. Completions
Fill in each blank with the correct word from the word list.
1. The boys left the park feeling _____ they were up for tonight's championship game.
2. This _____ will have you doing things you have never done before.
3. One of the boys offered Raymond _____
4. I can see Raymond's _____ in The Hook's face when he tries to hook.
5. At that time, we called it a case of_____
6. The lottery ticket paid $_____ to each winner.
7. Taking a last glimpse at the _____, Raymond slowly backed away from the garage.
8. The three talked about the championship game with _____
9. Gerald checked out the _____
10. He tightened up on Gerald's shirt and bounced his head several times on the _____

Air Jordans	car
confident	Porch
smoke	amnesia
Carver High School	marijuana
6,000	sound system

PART II: Writing Prompts
A. Write, describing the conversation between Raymond, his stepfather and Mr. Duncan.
B. If you were Raymond, how would you react after learning your parent or guardian hit the lottery for $6,000?
C. How would you make use of the money if your parent or guardian gave you part of the winnings?
D. Write, describing Raymond's reaction after learning he was given a car for a graduation gift.

PART III. Vocabulary
Use a dictionary to find the definition of the words in the word bank below.
Construct a new sentence for each word. Explain how they were used in Chapter 9.

Chapter Nine

Amnesia	marijuana
assist	quest
Confident	temporary
desperately	routine
Expression	scholarship
adjacent	lottery
Graduation	uplifting

PART IV: True/False
_____1. When Raymond arrived home, Gerald and some of his friends were sitting on the front porch playing chess.
_____2. One of the boys offered Raymond marijuana.
_____3. Raymond knocked the marijuana out of the boy's hand and shoved him into the hedges.
_____4. Raymond accepted the marijuana from the boy.
_____5. Gerald stated, "Benny D. is cool with me."
_____6. Mr. Duncan and Raymond's stepfather never attended Raymond's home games.
_____7. Mr. Duncan had never known Raymond's biological father.
_____8. The three talked about the championship game with the Chicago Bulls.
_____9. Raymond told Mr. Duncan he had no idea how he was going to stop The Hook.
_____10. Mr. Duncan was imitating Eddie Murphy

Chapter Ten

New uniforms
Police escort to the Coliseum
The starting five

The school bus that transported the team was parked in the gym's parking lot when the boys arrived.
"What time is it?" Raymond asked.
"Five fifty-three," Milton answered. The boys jumped out of the car and made a swift entrance through the gym doors. The Martin Luther King basketball team would wear new uniforms in tonight's game. This was a promise from Coach Mickey for their becoming contenders for the city's championship.

A vicious gold tiger stretched across the back of the warm-up jackets. The MLK insignia was embroidered at the top of the tiger's head. After a quick shower, the boys suited up in their new uniforms and made their way to the gym floor. The team was seated on the bleachers about midway in the gym. They were patiently waiting for player-coach Raymond Tinsley to assume leadership of the team.

"I don't have much to say fellows," Raymond began, "my only desire is to play the kind of game Coach Mickey would want us to play. As Coach Mickey said in the hospital, we have known this game plan all year. So, brothers, let's go out there and do it for Coach Mickey!"

"Get up on The Hook! Get up on The Hook!" was echoed in unison by members of the team.

"A win tonight not only makes us City Champs, but gives us a chance to compete for the state championship. The Gold! The Gold!" Milton shouted. The team continued talking about what coach Mickey would do in certain situations during the game." They were interrupted by the bus driver calling out to them from the far end of the gymnasium.

"Hey Raymond, we'd better leave now, traffic downtown is a mess this time of evening," she said.

Giving out high fives and flashing victory signs, the team boarded the yellow school bus for the trip to the Coliseum. The boys were a little surprised to see several police cars parked near their bus. The police escorted the bus to the Coliseum. Benny D. was still out there and they were taking no chances.

The MLK cheerleaders were waiting for their team's arrival at the player's entrance. "Get up on The Hook! GET UP ON THE HOOK!" they cheered. A large group of MLK fans standing near the entrance had joined in too. The team disembarked from the bus, raising their carrying bags above their heads.

This was Raymond's first time playing at the Coliseum. Traditionally, city championships were played in the Coliseum to accommodate the large crowd they generated. Former students from both schools had come from various parts of the USA to witness the championship game. Curtis Tinsley, Raymond's brother, was a former member of MLK's basketball team. He was a member of the team that defeated Carver six years ago for the city's championship title.

Chapter Ten

The rivalry between the two schools dated back twenty-eight years. Each year it gained momentum This was the seventh meeting of the two schools for this honor. Each team had three wins.

The Coliseum was practically filled to capacity when they made it to the playing court. The MLK Tigers formed two lines on the home side and began their warm-ups. Carver High's basketball team entered the Coliseum. Gold and blue pennants, ribbons, and noise makers created a spirited entrance for their team. The team passed through the two lines formed by the Carver cheerleaders and began their warm-ups. During the warm-ups, The Hook dunked several balls through the net. The Carver crowd roared insanely on each dunk. Both teams completed their warm ups and returned to the locker rooms.

"Hey Raymond, how do you feel, man?" Milton asked.

"Very loose, very loose," Raymond answered.

"Yeah, me too," replied Milton.

"Tigers, we've got ten minutes before returning to the floor." Together, as a team, they put together the starting five: guards - Milton, Aaron; forwards - Eric, Rafael; center - Raymond."

"Get up on The Hook! Get up on The Hook!" yelled the team in unison.

"Hey! Hey!" Kevin shouted, trying to make his shout heard over the team's shouts. "I have a short speech, a very short speech to make."

"Yeah, go on, Kevin." Raymond answered. "We are going to win this championship game for Coach Mickey and seniors on the team."

The team stood up and began yelling, "Go! R.T. . ., Get up on The Hook! Go! R.T., Get up on The Hook!"

"So Raymond, Eric, and Milton, we are going to send you guys off to college as city and state champs!"

"Get up on The Hook! Get up on The Hook!" the team yelled. Again, Raymond knew he had reached the mental plateau he needed for this game. He also knew his team was right there with him. They were ready together.

Activities

Understanding what you have read.
Do not irite in this book Use your Raymond Tinsley journal.

PART I. True/False
1. The bus that transported the team was not there when they returned to school.
2. The police escorted their bus to the Coliseum.
3. Raymond's older brother was a former member of the MLK basketball team.
4. The rivalry between the two schools dated back twenty-eight years.
5. It was the seventh meeting of the two schools competing for the city's championship.
6. During the warm-up, The Hook dunked several balls through the net.
7. Carver High School colors were Gold and Blue.
8. Kevin gave a pep talk before the team returned to the floor.
9. Raymond stated he would play the forward position the first quarter to confuse Carver.

PART II. Vocabulary
Use a dictionaiy to find the definition of the words listed below. Construct a new sentence for each word Explain how they were used in Chapter 10.

Accommodate	disembarked
Capacity	embroidered
Coliseum	insignia
Contenders	pennants
Dedicate	situations

PART III. Writing Prompts
Describe Kevin's emotional talk with the team.

Chapter Eleven

The tip-off
Passing the ball with accuracy
Raymond and Clarence, two tall trees reaching for the ceiling.

The championship game attracted over thirty thousand people. Yells from both schools were at an all time high when the teams returned to the court. After team introductions, Raymond and Clarence went to center court for the tip-off. Jumping about eight inches above The Hook's right hand, Raymond's left hand made the connection. Milton was on the receiving end of the tip. Milton held the ball high above his head.

"Move it!" Raymond yelled.

Each pass was accurate in testing Carver's defense. Aaron faked a move toward Milton but quickly passed the ball inside to Raymond. Raymond faked a swift move on The Hook. He shot a fall-away jump shot. Eric and Rafael had good positions under the basket for the rebound. Woosh! Two points! The MLK fans went wild. The guards from MLK were on Carver's end of the court before Raymond's ball hit the nets. This was to protect against Carver's well known fast breaks. This was one of the things Coach Mickey had drilled them on all year.

The Tigers set up for defense. The Carver High School Warriors brought the ball into enemy territory for the first time. The Warriors moved the ball with accuracy. A pass was made to The Hook. He faked a move on Raymond. Moving to his right with his right arm outstretched, he positioned himself for his hook shot. This was his best shot. Four out of five would fmd its way through the hoops. This was The Hook's first shot; Raymond had to stop it!

Timing Clarence's jump, he positioned himself in front of The Hook. He thought about Coach Mickey standing under the basket explaining how to stop this shot. Out of the corner of his eye, he could see The Hook positioning himself for the hook shot. Jumping very high, Raymond blocked the shot with his left hand. The ball deflected off the forehead of The Hook and into the hands of Eric Malone.

"A gift," he said looking up at Raymond and The Hook who both appeared to be two tall trees reaching for the ceiling in the Coliseum.

The fans were on their feet. "Get up on The Hook! Stay up on The Hook, Get up on The Hook! Stay up on The Hook!" was being shouted throughout the arena. Play continued. A quick pass to Aaron... a long lob to Rafael standing behind the three point line in the far right corner. Woosh! A three pointer for Rafael.

Carver put the ball in play. Carver faked a drive down the middle and passed off to a forward in the corner. Woosh! A three pointer for Carver. The three point play restored Carver's confidence. The Warriors initiated a full court press against the Tigers. A bad pass from Aaron ended up in the hands of a Carver player. A pass to The Hook. Woosh! Two points. Each team continued passing the ball with as much accuracy the opposing team would allow.

Raymond had held The Hook to nine points when the half-time buzzer sounded. Raymond had scored eleven points and made four assists.

Both teams talked strategy during the half-time break. Each was determined to win the championship game. The score was 31-28, MLK.

A commotion was taking place when the teams returned to the court. Police and security were chasing four men on the upper level in Section 8 on the Carver side. One of the men appeared to be Benny D. holding an automatic assault weapon above his head. He began firing shots in the air; tat, tat, tat, tat, tat, tat was the echoed sound of the weapon. Benny D. was jumping over people and firing his weapon repeatedly. He was trying to make it to the exit on the upper floor. This was the closest exit to the street.

It was a merging of the blue and gold and the gold and green on the basketball court. Both teams, cheerleaders, pep bands, referees, television and radio announcers were scrambling, trying to find safety from the gun fire. When Benny D. reached the floor, everyone had scattered for cover, with the exception of two players: **_Raymond Tinsley and Clarence Johnson, alias, The Hook._**

Understanding what you have read.
Do not write in this hook Use your Raymond Tinsley journal.

PART I. Completions
Fill in each blank with the correct word from the list below.
1. The championship game attracted over _____ people.
2. Raymond and _____ went to center court for the tip-off.
3. Each pass was _____ when testing Carver's defense.
4. Raymond blocked the shot with his ____ hand.
5. The Warriors initiated a full court _____ against the Tigers.
6. Both teams talked _____ during the half.
7. Police and security were chasing ____ men on the upper level on Carver's side.
8. One of the men appeared to be _____
9. When the man being chased by the police reached the floor, every body had scattered with the exception of two players; _____ and _____

assault	left	Benny D.
press	Clarence	Raymond
four	strategy	accurate
The Hook	eight	30,000

PART I. Vocabulary
Use a dictionary to find the definition for the words listed below. Explain how each was used in Chapter 11. Write a new sentence for each word.

accurate
confidence
alias
determined
arena
introduction
commotion
merging

PART III. Writing Prompts
A. The Hook scored nine points in the first half. Do you think Raymond's strategy for guarding The Hook is effective?
B. If you were Raymond, what would you say to the team during the half time break?

49

C. In Chapter 6, Raymond's stepfather described Benny D. as a psychotic drug dealer. Write your personal reaction of Benny D.
D. Use a dictionary to find the definition for the word psychotic.

Chapter Twelve

The big chase
The capture of Benny D.
The five-second play

Scholarship recipients

Laughing hysterically and babbling incoherently and firing into the air, Benny D. was nearing the exit. "Not this time," Raymond thought. He began running in the direction of Benny D. The Hook also joined in the chase of the erratic Benny D. Benny D. had one foot out the exit door before Raymond and The Hook caught up to him. Hitting him hard and high, Raymond knocked the weapon out of his hand. At the same time, The Hook knocked Benny D.'s legs from under him. This left him spinning like a wheel. Biff! Wham! Bam! was the sound of the lefts and rights from Raymond landing solid punches to Benny D.'s stomach and head. Raymond had boxed him to the center of the floor before security and police were able to pull him off of Benny D. When the fans saw what was going on, they slowly returned to their seats. No way were they going to miss the rest of this game.

The Hook and Raymond stood at center court waiting for the tip-off to start the second half. He turned and shook The Hook's hand and said, " ain't over yet, brother."

The Hook replied, "Let's start the show!"

The crowd got back into the game. Benny D. was history. "It's time to play some ball," Raymond shouted to his team.

This time Carver controlled the tip. Moving the ball quickly, Carver setup their offensive attack. An alley-oop to The Hook with both hands high above the rim to receive the ball. Whoosh. . . two points for The Hook. The Warriors began the full court press on the Tigers. This made it difficult for the Tigers to inbound the ball. The Warriors were calling out coded defensive signals. A bad inbound pass from the Tigers landed in the hands of a Warrior. Next, a quick pass to The Hook standing left of Raymond. The Hook faked a jump shot. Then taking a long stride with his right foot, he went into the hook shot position. Raymond couldn't block the shot. Whoosh! Two more points for The Hook. Both teams continued executing the ball with accuracy. Both teams kept the full court press until the last three minutes of the game.

With six seconds left in the game, the Warriors were out in front, 68 - 67. The Tigers called a time-out. "All right Tigers, this is it," Raymond began. The team formed a circle around him and listened attentively even though everyone knew which play they would use: the five-second play, code named R.T. "Okay you guys, let's go do it for the coach," Raymond concluded.

In unison, the Tigers shouted, "For the Coach." The buzzer sounded. Both teams returned to the court. The crowd was tense. Complete silence from both MLK and Carver fans. At the sound of the whistle, Aaron passed the ball in to Eric. Eric quickly lobbed the ball to Raymond standing to the left of The Hook. The Hook was two feet from the basket.

Raymond faked a double jump shot on The Hook He went under the basket and dunked a two hand shot over his back for the points. The fiberglass backboard cracked after the shot The popping of the nets sent a piercing sound to the ears of Carver fans. The buzzer sounded "The ga-am-m-ee is over," the announcer said, "Martin Luther King, 69, George Washington Carver, 68." MLK fans from both sides of the floor swarmed to center court They were chanting, "We're number one! We're number one! We're number one!" Carver fans quietly left the Coliseum, trying to figure out what had happened.

It was difficult for the team to return to the dressing room. The news media and dedicated fans from both sides were swarming around the Tigers. Finally reaching the dressing room, the scout from UCLA was patiently waiting to talk to seniors on the MLK team.

The coaching staff and team members from Carver entered the dressing room.

The Carver team congratulated the Tigers and wished them well in the state play-offs.

The Hook shook hands with Raymond. Both boys admitted it was a tough game.

The mayor presented the winning trophy to the MLK team. Raymond accepted on behalf of his team. Hands right over left, the team sang the school song.

Steve Barnes, the UCLA scout, offered Raymond, Milton, and The Hook full basketball scholarships. "All right," the boys shouted going through high fives and the approval handshake.

The Hook is not a bad guy after all, Raymond thought. "Did I really go up on The Hook?"

Activities

Understanding what you have read.
Do not write in this book Use your Raymond Tinsley journal.

PART I. True/False
1. Raymond and Milton tackled Benny D. at the exit door.
2. The Hook watched from center court.
3. The game was postponed an hour after they captured Benny D.
4. Raymond and The Hook accepted scholarships to UCLA.
5. The coach and team from Carver congratulated the Tigers.

PART II. Completions
Fill in each blank with correct word from the word list to complete the sentence.
1. Benny D. had one foot out the door before Raymond and _____ caught up to him.
2. The MLK's code name for the five second play was _____
3. MLK won the championship game by _____ point.
4. _____ offered Raymond, Milton, and Clarence full _____ to UCLA.
5. Raymond thought, "Did I really get up on_____

The Hook
scholarships
Clarence
Steve Barnes
one
R.T.

PART III. Vocabulary
Use a dictionary to find the definition of the words listed below. Construct a new sentence for each word. Explain how it was used in Chapter 12.

Attentively	defensive
fiberglass	lobbed
chanting	Erratic
hysterically	offensive
congratulated	executing
Incoherently	scholarship

PART IV. Know Your Characters
Fill in each blank with a word from the word list to answer the question.
1. ____ The physics teacher
2. ____ The friend of Raymond's stepfather
3. ____ The man who was with Raymond's biological father before he was killed.
4. ____ The musician
5. ____ The track star from Malcolm X High School
6. ____ Won eight gold medals in the 1941 Olympics
7. ____ The insane drug dealer
8. ____ The player making the three point play from the corner
9. ____ The player receiving the gift
10. ____ The fine gymnast

A. Benny D.	B. Darrell
C. Jesse Owens	D. Mr. Bates
E. Mr. Harper	F. Cassandra Hawkins
G. Eric	H. Milton
I. Mr. Duncan	J. Rafael

PART VI. *Personal Reactions*
A. Raymond called Coach Mickey after the game at Somerest Memorial Hospital to tell him of the win over Carver High School.

What you would say to Coach Mickey if you were Raymond?

UNIT III TEST
Chapters 9-12

MIDTERM

Name_____ Score_____ Homeroom_____

PART I. True/False (50 points)

_____ 1. Mr. Duncan knew Raymond's real father before he was killed in the attempted liquor store robbery.
_____ 2. Mr. Duncan bragged about the $5 million dollar contract with the Chicago Bears.
_____ 3. Raymond loved the motorcycle his mom and dad gave him for graduation.
_____ 4. Gerald hit the lottery for $6,000.
_____ 5. Raymond blacked out when they told him about the winning ticket.
_____ 6. The bus that transported the team was not there when they arrived back at school.
_____ 7. The police escorted the bus to the coliseum.
_____ 8. Raymond's older brother was a former member of the MLK basket ball team.
_____ 9. The rivalry between the two schools dated back twenty-eight years.
_____ 10. Raymond and Milton tackled Benny D. at the exit door.
_____ 11. The Hook watched from center court.
_____ 12. The game was postponed an hour after they captured Benny D.
_____ 13. Raymond and The Hook accepted scholarships to UCLA.
_____ 14. The coach and the team from Carver congratulated the Tigers.
_____ 15. It was the seventh meeting of the two schools competing for the city's championship.
_____ 16. During the warm-up, The Hook dunked several balls through the net.
_____ 17. The Carver High School colors were Gold and Blue.
_____ 18. Kevin gave a pep talk before the team returned to the floor.
_____ 19. Raymond stated that he would play the forward position the first quarter to confuse Carver.
_____ 20. Mr. Thomas led the school song.
_____ 21. When Raymond arrived home, Gerald and some of his friends were sitting on the front porch playing dominoes.
_____ 22. One of the boys offered Raymond marijuana.
_____ 23. Raymond knocked the marijuana out of the boy's hand and shoved him into the hedges.
_____ 24. Raymond told Gerald that marijuana only adds to the problem
_____ 25. Gerald was drug free.

PART II. Completions (20 points)
1. The championship game attracted over _____ people.
2. Raymond and _____ went to center court for the tip-off.
3. Each pass was _____ when testing Carver's defense.
4. Raymond blocked the shot with his _____ hand.
5. Police and security were chasing four men on the upper level in Section _____ on Carver's side.
6. One of the men appeared to be _____
7. _____ was jumping over people and firing an assault weapon into the air.
8. When the man being chased by the police reached the floor, everybody had scattered with the exception of two players, _____ and _____.
9. MLK's code name for the five second play was _____
10. MLK won the game by _____ point(s).

A. Benny D. B. eight
C. 30,000   D. The Hook
E. left   F. one
F. Steve Barnes G. Raymond
H. R.T.   H. Accurate

PART III. Know Your Characters (20 points)
_____ 1. The drug dealer
_____ 2. Clarence Johnson
_____ 3. College scout
_____ 4. Raymond's best friend
_____ 5. Knew Raymond's real father
_____ 6. Led team fight song
_____ 7. Gave a pep talk
_____ 8. Raymond's brother
_____ 9. Escorted bus to the /Coliseum
_____ 10. The player making the three point play from the corner

A. Steve Barnes
B. Milton
C. BennyD
D. Mr. Duncan
E. The Hook
F. Rafael
G. Police
H. Mr. Thomas
I. Kevin
J. Gerald

Part IV. Writing Prompt (10 points)
After capturing Benny D., Raymond and Clarence went to center floor for the tip off. Raymond turned and shook The Hook's hand and said, "It am 't over yet brother." The Hook replied, "Let's start the show."
A. What is your impression of this short conversation between the boys?

Chapter Thirteen

Getting ready for UCLA
The California rap
It's party time
We would never do anything to blow our scholarships
The lethal salad fork
Watery red eyes and slow speech make it obvious

Ebony girls on the beach

The MLK Tigers won the state 4A basketball championship. Coach Mickey recovered from the gunshot wounds in time to travel with the team to the state capitol.

The summer rolled around pretty fast as Raymond, Clarence, and Milton prepared for their freshman year at UCLA. The family gave a house party and invited the coach and team. A good time was shared by all.

"It takes brains to be a good basketball player, and you boys are both smart. But remember, the purpose of going to college is to get a good education," Coach Mickey said to the boys.

"We know, coach," answered Raymond as he went through the high five with him.

Don't forget to take your Malcolm-X pull-over; it gets cold sometimes at night in California," Raymond's mother shouted from the kitchen.

"Mamma, California is the state with those fme ebony sisters, sunshine, beaches, and movie stars," Raymond answered.

"That's right," Milton interrupted as he began the *California rap:*
We're on our way to college to get an education
And to improve our skills in female communication.
I'm gonna play ball, and major in law
And maybe get some brothers out of jail in Arkansas.
Listen up everybody, I don't wanna be bold
But we gotta have some fun as we reach for our goaL
California, California is the place I wanna be
With the pretty beach girls going crazy over me.

Coming out of the kitchen with a long wooden salad fork in her hand, Raymond's mother walked directly towards Milton, waving the fork left to right around his head, and expressing herself calmly and emphatically. "This is just what I am afraid of. Beaches, girls, Hollywood, and everything else there will take your minds off your studies."

"Raymond Tinsley, I will come to UCLA and drown you and those ebony girls on the beach, and put out a distress signal for JAWS! You know what I'm saying? Raymond Tinsley!" she shouted as she started humming the theme music from the motion picture, "Jaws". Mrs. Tinsley had a habit of calling Raymond by his full name when she was getting her point across.

"I know, Mom. Milton is just talking and saying things. We know what we have to do. We would never do anything to blow our scholarships and jeopardize our chances of not completing college," Raymond answered.

"Mrs. Tinsley, I plan to make the Dean's List each semester," Milton winced as he watched the salad fork circling around his head.

"Well, it is best you make the Dean's List rather than my list!" Raymond's mother answered waving the salad fork at both of them.

Laughing hard at watching Raymond and Milton react to Mrs. Tinsley's verbal chastising, Coach Mickey had to pretend he was choking on the punch and cheese covered Ritz crackers he was eating to keep from giving himself away. Afterwards, they all had a good laugh.

Gerald came into the room with three of his friends. It appeared that all four had been using drugs. Watery, red eyes and slow speech made it obvious.

"What's up,? What's up? Gerald mumbled as he walked towards Raymond with his left hand extended. Since the tragic death of his father, Gerald had resorted to drugs and gangbanging. He had dropped out of school and had been arrested twice for drug possession. It was no secret. Everyone in the room knew about Gerald's activities. Raymond's mother caught Gerald by the arm and escorted him to the kitchen.

"You are not going to break up this party," she said. Turning to Gerald, she waved the same salad fork with which she had threatened Milton and Raymond.

"Aw, Mom, go slow! Don't be so hard on me. I am not going to do anything to upset this little old party," answered Gerald talking incoherently and trying to maintain his balance by leaning on the kitchen sink.

Mrs. Tinsley was tempted to go-off on him. She knew if she did, the party would be over. She managed to get control over her anger as Raymond and Milton walked into the kitchen. Raymond quickly escorted Gerald out of the kitchen to the backyard. Gerald knew if his mother went off on him, the entire neighborhood would witness the event.

Gerald sat on an old Goodyear tire leaning against the garage. Raymond stood directly in front of Gerald loudly chastising Gerald about his drug habit, gangbanging, his friends, his poor attendance at school, and his failing grades.

Milton walked around to the alley where Mr. Duncan was sitting in his van watching the NBA playoff games. Mr. Duncan was a true fan of Raymond and Milton. He and Raymond's stepfather attended all of their home games. He watched the two grow up together, and had followed their sports since day one of high school. Mr. Duncan and Milton talked about his scholarship to UCLA and his dreams of becoming a superstar.

"Hey Milton, let's get back to the party, I think Gerald has gotten himself together," Raymond said. Gerald appeared to have control of himself after the talk with Raymond. They said good-bye to Mr. Duncan, and the three boys returned to the party. Gerald's partners had immediately left the party when Raymond took Gerald out in the backyard because one of them remembered Raymond's anger and treatment when he offered Raymond marijuana. They wanted no part of Raymond's anger.

Activities

Understanding what you have read.
Do not write in this book Use your Raymond Tinsley journal

PART I. True/False
1. Coach Mickey was still in the hospital recovering from the gunshot wounds.
2. MLK lost to Carver in the state championship game.
3. Mrs. Tinsley told Raymond she would understand if he fell behind in his studies.
4. Coach Mickey laughed so hard that he had to pretend he was choking on the chicken and beer.
5. Gerald's partners were drug users.
6. Gerald's partners remained at the party until it was over.
7. Mr. Duncan was watching the super bowl game in his van.
8. Raymond never talked to Gerald about his drug problem.
9. Gerald was a junior at Carver High School.
10. Raymond knew if Mrs. Tinsley had gotten upset with Gerald; the neighborhood would know about it.

PART II. Vocabulary
Use a dictionary to find the definition of the words below. Construct a new sentence for each word Explain how the word was used in Chapter 13.

attendance	ebony
incoherently	obvious
calmly	education
jeopardize	resorted
chastising	emphatically
lethal	threatened
communication	immediately
marijuana	tragic

PART III. Personal Reactions
Discuss
A. If you were Raymond, what would you say to Gerald about his use of drugs and gang activities?
B. In his California rap, why do you think Milton rapped about getting some brothers out of jail in Arkansas?
C. Why did Mrs. Tinsley threaten Milton and Raymond with the wood salad fork?
D. Why did what Raymond's mother say to him and Milton cause Coach Mickey to laugh so hard?

PART IV Writing Prompts
Write and characterize a short skit about Mrs. Tinsley, Raymond, Milton and the salad fork

Chapter Fourteen

When they kissed, two little girls behind them said, "Stop that!"

Raymond was up early the next morning for his daily workout at the Jesse Owens Park. When he returned home, he made a phone call to Cassandra Hawkins; the fine track star from Malcolm-X High School.

After a few rings, a soft voice answered, "Hello."

"Hello, may I speak with Cassandra, please," Raymond asked?

"Raymond? Raymond Tinsley? Is this the real Raymond Tinsley? Star-r-rr center from MLK High School?" Cassandra teased.

"Yeah, what's up Cassandra?" Raymond asked. "I'm getting ready for school.

You know, I leave next Thursday. Maybe we can hook-up and fly out together," Raymond said.

"Sounds good to me," she responded.

"I'm going to the mall this afternoon to do some school shopping. Do you want to meet me there? Perhaps we could go to a movie." Raymond suggested.

"Okay, what time R.T.?" she asked.

"Mmmm, about three," he answered.

"Okay, I'll meet you in front of Montgomery Ward at three," she answered. "Bye."

When Raymond hung up the phone, he fell to his knees and shouted, "Y-YE-ES-S!" His mother knocked on his door and inquired whether he was all right.

"Hey, I'm okay, mom! I just received some good news."

"Well, I hope you don't receive any more while I'm here," she smiled.

Raymond changed clothes and drove to First Chicago Bank where he had a savings account. He had started saving when he first began working at Slap Burgers. He had about seven hundred dollars in his account for new clothes and other personal items he needed for college.

When he returned from the bank, his mother told him he had received a call from Dr. Healy, UCLA's Physical Education Department. "I wrote the information down. It's on the dining room table," she said.

Raymond immediately returned the call. "Dr. Healy's office," the voice on the other end answered.

"This is Raymond Tinsley returning Dr. Healy's call," he stated.

"Just a moment please."

Raymond had no idea what this call was about. He had talked with the coaching staff on several occasions, but never to a Dr. Healy. "Hello Raymond, this is Dr. Healy, head of the Physical Education Department at UCLA. How are you?" he asked.

"Fine, sir, and yourself?

"Doing okay. The reason I'm calling is to invite you to the retreat this weekend in Malibu. Every year, the physical Education Department sponsors a weekend retreat for athletes attending UCLA. It gives freshmen athletes an opportunity to meet other athletes who are participating in sports different from their own. This is a volunteer event, and you are not required to attend. I know that you are not scheduled to report until next week, but this is a wonderful opportunity for you to meet your peers before the pressures of school begin. I know this is a short notice, but the orientation you will receive at the retreat will be useful. Do you think you will be able to attend?" Dr. Healy asked.

"That's difficult to answer at this time. It sounds terrific, and I'd certainly like to attend, but I'm not sure I can change my reservations in time. I will call you back tomorrow," Raymond answered.

"Good," Dr. Healy said, I expect to hear from you tomorrow morning, then. Good-bye.'

After hanging up from Dr. Healy, Raymond thought about the promise he had made to Cassandra regarding flying together next Thursday. This was a decision he had to make before tomorrow.

At 2:30, Raymond left for the mall, driving the car his mom had given him for graduation. He arrived at 2:47. He was glad to be early. He didn't want to late for his first date with Cassandra. He later found out Cassandra had been waiting for him since 2:30.

The two shopped and talked for two hours. Then they went to Loew's Theater. Raymond and Cassandra were so busy talking about college and seriously getting acquainted, they went into Studio A instead of Studio B. Studio B was the one showing Amistad, the movie they wanted to see.

They didn't realize it until they saw Snow White and the seven dwarfs appear on the screen. A double feature of Walt Disney's Snow White and Cinderella was showing in Studio A. The two had a good laugh. They decided to sit through both movies anyhow. Cassandra made a point that she has always enjoyed the ending of Snow White; especially the part where she gets awakened by her prince in shinning armor.

"Yeah, yeah, he was right on time," Raymond said.

"I think you are right on time in my life too, Raymond Tinsley," Cassandra said as she reached for Raymond's hand. Simultaneously, all four of their hands came together. A moment of silence blanketed the theater. There was a sparkle in Cassandra's eyes. They glowed in the dark After a moment, they turned to each other, and, and, and... and,... kissed

Two little girls sitting behind Raymond and Cassandra went, "Mmmmmmm! Now, you go girl!"

Raymond and Cassandra had failed to realize that eighty-five percent of the audience were children. After the movie, they walked behind Raymond and Cassandra saying, "Mmmmmmm !"

When they arrived outside, a commotion was taking place in the parking lot adjacent to the theater. Several boys were pointing toward a group of boys near the south end of the lot. Suddenly! A volley of gunfire could be heard from the south end of the lot. People scattered for cover. Raymond and Cassandra took cover behind the ticket booth. The boys at the south end of the lot sped away in a low- riding '84 Chevy.

After the shooting, people gathered around a person who had been wounded by the cross-fire between the two gangs. Raymond and Cassandra walked over to the crowd and discovered it was one of the little girls sitting behind them in the theater.

Raymond and Cassandra ran over to see what they could do.

"Has anyone called the police and an ambulance?" he asked. When nobody answered, he asked Cassandra to go and call. In the meantime, he looked to see if he could stop the bleeding. Someone offered a large handkerchief, and he pressed it against the wound, trying not to hurt the little girl.

Someone else suggested they should move her to a more comfortable spot, but Raymond told them it would be better not to move her until professional care came. He asked if anyone had something to cover her with, because, warm as it was, he was afraid that she might go into shock from the wound. Someone in the crowd produced a light sweater.

Just about then Cassandra called the police from her cell. Paramedics arrived a few minutes later. When they were sure everything was being taken care of and that the little girl would be all right, they left.

Activities

Understanding what you have read.
Do not rite in this book Use your Raymond Tinsley journal

PART I. Word Meaning
Use a dictionary to find the definition of the words listed below. Report your findings to the class. Construct a sentence on how each word relates to Chapter 14.

Adjacent   commotion
retreat   scattered
blanketed   orientation
resources   volley

PART II Discussions
A. If you had money and resources, what would you do to protect kids from being killed, or wounded by rival gangs?
B. Describe and write your personal feelings about the little girl being wounded accidentally by rival gangs.
C. Describe what you think are the feelings of the parents of the little girl who was wounded.
D. Do you think the people responsible for the shooting will be apprehended?
Give an explanation for your answer.

Part. III   Reading Graphs and Tables

Directions: This is a test of your ability to read a table. Write the correct answer in your Raymond Tinsley journal.

August

Sunday	Monday	Tuesday	Wednesday	Thursday	Friday	Saturday
				1	2	3
4	5	6	7	8	9	10
11	12	13	14	15	16	17
18	19	20	21	22	23	24
25	26	27	28	29	30	31

1. What is the date of the second Tuesday in August?

A. August 22	B. August 6	C. August 13	D. August 30	E. August 9

2. Which of the seven days comes five times in the month?

A. Monday, Tuesday, Wednesday	B. Friday, Saturday, Sunday	C. Thursday, Friday, Saturday	D. Wednesday, Thursday, Friday	E. Tuesday, Wednesday, Saturday

3. Cassandra told Raymond she planned to leave for Los Angeles a week from tomorrow. If today's date is Wednesday, August 14 what is the day and date Cassandra will leave for Los Angeles, California?

A. Tuesday August 20	B. Thursday August 22	C. Thursday August 29	D. Friday August 30

Raymond told Dr. Healy he would not be able to attend the weekend retreat for UCLA athletes on the third Thursday of August. What is the date of the weekend retreat?

    A. August 22   B. August 15   C. August 29

5. Freshman orientation starts the second Tuesday in August. What is the date?
    A. August 8   B. August 13   C. August 22

PART IV. True/False
1. Cassandra and Raymond had scholarships to the same college.
2. Cassandra asked Raymond to meet her in front of Foot Locker.
3. The two little girls that saw Raymond and Cassandra kissing told them to stop.
4. Raymond told Dr. Healy he would attend the retreat.
5. Raymond jumped out of the window after Cassandra told him to meet her at Foot Locker.

Chapter Fifteen

The prevention and intervention program at the park

On the way home, Cassandra and Raymond talked about the gang problem in the neighborhood. After dropping Cassandra off at home, Raymond returned home, and called Milton to tell him what happened at the theater.

The boys discussed the gang problem and what was being done to stop the violence. They wondered what they could do because Raymond could not stop thinking about the little girl who had been wounded at the theater.

Milton told Raymond he knew of a program at the Jesse Owens Park that was created as an alternative to gang activities. They decided to find out more about the program. Remembering how The Hook went after Benny D. at the championship game, Raymond thought it would be a good idea for them to talk to him, and they did.

The next day, they picked Clarence up, and the three of them went to the park. Upon arriving, Raymond immediately recognized the director; he and Curtis, Raymond's older brother, played ball together at MLK. Jeffrey Cunningham, the director, was a senior at Chicago State University. He did volunteer work at the park during school months. He was employed by the Chicago Parks and Recreation Department during the summer.

Jeffrey was in a meeting with his summer staff when they arrived. His staff consisted of black and Hispanic college students home for summer vacation. Jeffrey managed to have the gangs agree to a truce while they were on park grounds; therefore, in some of the sports programs offered at the park, rival gangs could compete peacefully against each other. Through sports, a dialogue was established between rival gangs.

Violence in and near the park dropped dramatically. Adolescents involved in sports they enjoy are less likely to engage in gang activities. Jeffrey had a good program that was making a difference in the lives of black and Hispanic adolescents.

"Raymond, Raymond Tinsley," Jeffrey said, getting up from the table and shaking Raymond's hand.

"Hey Jeffrey, what's up? I told my friends I thought I knew you."

"How could you forget me when your brother and I were the badest dudes to ever wear a MLK uniform? We were state champs two years straight. . . okay!" the smiling Jeff said.

"I know, I know. Curtis reminds me all the time." Raymond answered.

"Say man, I want you to meet my summer staff," he continued. "Who are the brothers with you?"

"This is Milton and Clarence. The three of us will be attending UCLA this fall." Raymond answered.

"That's all right. It's going to take brothers like you three to show kids the streets are not where it's at. Come on over, I want you all to meet the staff."

They all moved towards the conference table and Jeffrey made the introductions. "Around the table from my left are Louis Hernandez, Roland Hunt, Jesslyn Bibbs, Maria Gonzales, James Tate, Patricia Gates, and Cedrick Woods.

Chapter Fifteen

"People, meet Raymond, Clarence, and Milton. These brothers will be playing ball for UCLA this fall." Jeffrey went on to explain the prevention and intervention program.

Jeffrey's program was so effective, it had become a model for Chicago's Park Districts Recreation Programs. Parks adopting this program had shown a decrease in random violence and gang activities. Before this program was put in place, 70% of the clients felt that gang activities would increase. After participating in the program, only 28% felt that gang activities would increase. And indeed, random violence and gang activities had decreased in those parks. Raymond, Milton and Clarence agreed to work with kids during their school breaks, and summer months.

Raymond left the park feeling better about what was being done to stop the violence. He also recognized that the success Jeffrey's program was creating was brought about by starting a dialogue between the gang factions in conjunction with making available to gang members organized activities that kids, gang members included, enjoyed.

Raymond dropped Milton off and returned home to make the call to Dr. Healy. Raymond explained to Dr. Healy he could not attend the weekend retreat for UCLA athletes. He told him about the parks' program and said he wanted to spend the time left working with Jeffrey Cunningham in the prevention and intervention program at Jesse Owens Park

Activities

Understanding what you have read.
Do not write in this book Use your Raymond Tinsley journal.

PART I True/False
 1. On the way home, Raymond and Cassandra talked about the flight to California.
 2. Cassandra and Raymond realized the urgency to stop kids from killing kids.
 3. After dropping Cassandra off at home, Raymond called Milton on his car phone.
 4. The boys decided to find out more about the prevention and intervention program at Jesse Owns Park.
 5. They picked up Eric Malone on the way to the park.
 6. Jeffrey Cunningham played ball with Milton's brother for MLK High School.
 7. Jeffrey Cunningham was a senior at Malcolm X High School.
 8. When they arrived at the park, they located Jeffrey in a staff meeting.
 9. The staff consisted only of black male college students.
10. The three boys left the park learning very little about the prevention and intervention program.
11. Before the program, 70% of the clients felt that gang activities would increase.
12. After the program started, 28% felt that gang activities would increase.
13. Only Raymond agreed to work in the prevention and intervention program.
14. The gangs established a dialogue through sports.
15. A truce was declared while participating in park activities.
16. Before leaving for college, Raymond wanted to spend some of his time with the prevention and intervention program.
17. Adolescents participating in an activity they enjoy are less likely to destroy property or themselves.
18. Raymond told Dr. Healy he would attend the weekend retreat.
19. The program at Jesse Owens Park was a model for other parks.
20. Thoughts and feelings about the little girl wounded in the crossfire would not go away.

PART IL Vocabulary
Use a dictionary to find the definition of words listed below. Construct a New sentence for each word. Explain how they were used in Chapter 15.

adopt (adopting)	model
intervention	volunteer
alternative	prevention
declared	retreat
dialogue	staff

director	truce
dramatically	urgency
factions	violence

PART III Class Discussions

Discuss the following questions. Give explanations for your answers.

A. Why do you think Raymond wanted to learn more about the prevention and intervention program?
B. Why do you think the staff included Hispanic Americans?
C. Why do you think the program was successful?
D. Why do you think the boys agreed to work with the program during the summer months and school breaks?

Activities cont.   Chapter 15

Part IV. *Using Your Skills: Reading a Circle Graph*

A GROWING PARTICIPATION
IN RECREATIONAL ACTIVITIES AT THE PARK

BEFORE THE TOURNAMENT

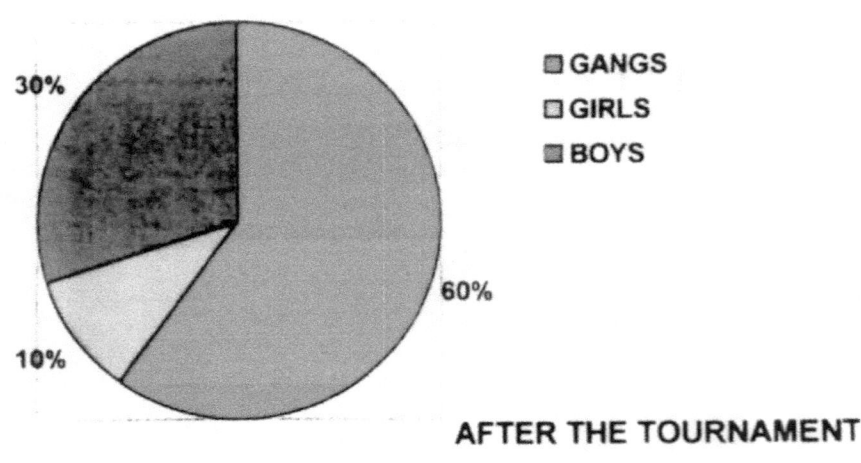

AFTER THE TOURNAMENT

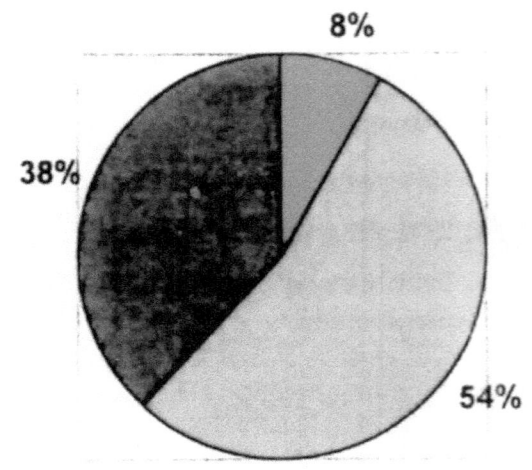

Chapter Fifteen

1. In the graphs, gang activity is represented by
   A. Red
   B. Green
   C. Blue

2. According to the graphs, what percentage of kids participated in gang activities before the clinic and tournament?
   A. 10%
   B. 60%
   C. 30%

3. According to the graph, gang activities decreased by how many percentage points after the clinic and tournament?
   A. 8%
   B. 46%
   C. 52%

4. According to the graphs, the participation of neighborhood girls in recreational activities in the park increased by how many percentage points after the tournament.
   A. 52% B. 44% C. 8%

5. According to the graphs, which of the following statements is accurate?
   A. Neighborhood girls had the greatest percentage of participation before the clinic and tournament
   B. Neighborhood boys had the greatest percentage of participation after the clinic and tournament.
   C. Gang activities decreased rapidly after the tournament.

Chapter Sixteen

The drive to California
The Interstate showdown in Arizona
Slap Burgers, 52 miles ahead, exit 27A

Raymond and his mother agreed he would not take the car until he completed the first semester of his freshmen year satisfactorily. Raymond wanted to do well. His mother thought the car would be a distraction. Adjusting to college life was going to be hard enough without having wheels just sitting around waiting to be driven.

"After all," she said, "if you need transportation, Milton can take his car."

Raymond's stepfather felt just the opposite. It turned out that Milton's car really belonged to his mother who needed it. Besides, he doubted that Milton's car was in good enough condition to make that long a trip. He thought Raymond had reached a level of maturity to make the adjustment with or without the car. He also knew that Raymond wanted very much to take the car but was honoring his mother's request not to take it.

Driving across country was another concern of hers. On Thursday, a week before school, the three talked about the car. Raymond's mother put up a good fight. However, she agreed when Raymond's stepfather offered to drive to California with Raymond and fly back home.

"I guess it is time for a mother to let go," Mrs. Tinsley said apprehensively. She was remembering reading last year of a student driving to college and not being heard from since.

"This is a repeat of your child going to school for the first time. These are the same fears you felt when he went to kindergarten," Raymond's stepfather said.

"This is a giant step for Raymond, but I know he can handle it."

"Is Milton going with you?" his mom inquired.

"I'm sure he would like to, but I don't know about his mother."

"What is Milton's number?" I am going to talk to his mother of about this driving to California." Mrs. Tinsley talked to Milton 's mom two hours on the phone.

"Girl I know what you are saying. It is dangerous on the interstates, uh, hun, yeah, girl, I know what you mean. Uh, huh, girl please!" she said. Milton's mother could talk. AT&T could definitely use her in one of their commercials; her true voice comes through loud and clear. "Girl, I am happy for them, California is all Milton has been talking about. Girl, I have five kids, I wish they could all go somewhere," she said.

The next few days were spent getting ready for the drive to California. The Chicago Motor Club of the American Automobile Association mapped their route including rest stops. The three left on a Tuesday morning at 3 a.m. Luggage was shipped by Greyhound. Raymond's father drove the first leg. Sixteen hours

Chapter Sixteen

later, they were in Amarillo, Texas, where they spent the night. The next day was spent getting out of Texas and driving through New Mexico.

Raymond's stepfather was asleep on the back seat when they reached the State of Arizona. He was snoring so hard that Milton plugged in his portable radio's earphones. The snoring didn't bother Raymond; he had been hearing it for years. They were getting close to Flagstaff; billboards were coming up pretty fast. Slap Burgers, 52 Miles, Exit 22A. Looking in the rear view mirror, Raymond noticed an Arizona Highway Patrol car behind him. It had been trailing him for quite some time. This didn't bother Raymond because he knew he wasn't breaking any laws. He was driving within the speed limit. Raymond noticed another patrol car making a U- turn and following the first car.

"Hey! Milton!" reaching over pulling one of the earphones from Milton's ear, Raymond said, "I think we are going to be pulled over."

Milton viewed the patrol cars through the rear view mirror. "Yeah, you might be right. They sure are checking us out."

The next instant Raymond saw the spinning red lights in his rear view mirror. The sudden change in speed awakened Raymond's stepfather. Watching through the rear view 'mirrors, Raymond could see the officers get out of their cars with their hands on their revolvers. The second patrol car pulled in front of them.

These officers also approached them with hands on their revolvers. By this time, Raymond's dad was wide awake on the back seat. "Keep your hands where they can see them. We don't want to be shot accidentally."

"Good evening, my name is Officer Bundy, would the three of you step out of the car, please."

The three got out and moved to the rear of the car.

"Where are you headed," one of the officers asked.

Before Raymond could answer, his stepfather intervened, "Were we speeding? Is something mechanically wrong with our car?" he asked. His questions were ignored and they were asked for identification.

Other officers on the scene began looking through the car. During this time, two more patrol cars arrived on the scene, including a captain. They knew not to say anything or make any abrupt moves. They couldn't count the number of times they had been pulled over because they were black adolescents wearing their caps differently. Accordingly, all black males are involved in drugs and gangs.

A black family had stopped to witness what was going on. One of the children began videotaping the incident. When one of the officers observed the camera, he summoned the captain. The captain didn't like this because they had no justifiable reason nor had they found justifiable reason during their search to have pulled them over. Initiating correct police procedures, the captain told Raymond's dad everything checked out okay and that they could go.

"Pulling us over the way you did was humiliating. Still, we allowed you to do your job. But, you made a mistake, and you owe us an apology. I hope your pride allows you to do right by us and apologize," he retorted.

Suddenly the captain's demeanor changed. "I know how you feel sir, but we have a dangerous job to do. Sometimes its difficult to distinguish the good guys from the bad guys."

The other officers gathered around to hear their conversation. "We had just received a bulletin from Albuquerque that two black males robbed a Taco Bell and may be headed in this direction, and at first we couldn't tell there were three men in your car," he continued. We don't get too many young black men driving this road, so we thought it prudent to check out this lead. We were wrong and I do apologize for our mistake."

"Well, I can understand. I just hope you take every opportunity you have to recall this experience and share it with your fellow officers. All black male adolescents are not bad. Their attire may be different from yours and they may wear their hats in different ways, but that doesn't make them criminals. These young brothers are on their way to college–UCLA." Raymond's dad said. Having said that, they got back in their car and the officers dispersed.

"Come on, Dad, let's move on!" Raymond said with a note of discouragement in his voice. "We can make Flagstaff before nightfall." They put the car back on the road and headed west.

Activities

Understanding what you have read.
Do not write in this hook Use your Rajmond Tinsley journal.

PART I True/False
1. Raymond and his mother agreed he would not take the car to college until he satisfactorily completed his freshmen year.
2. Raymond knew he had to do well his freshman year.
3. Raymond's stepfather felt Raymond would make the adjustment with or without the car.
4. Driving across country was a major concern of Mrs. Tinsley.
5. She only agreed to his taking the car after Raymond's stepfather said he would go with him.
6. Mrs. Tinsley and Milton's mother talked approximately two hours on the phone.
7. The American Automobile Association mapped their routes and rest stops to California.
8. Raymond drove the first leg.
9. Sixteen hours after leaving home, they stayed over night in Flagstaff, Arizona.
10. Milton was snoring so hard Raymond had to use his radio earphones.
11. Raymond knew they were getting close to Los Angeles; the fast food billboards were coming up pretty fast.
12. In the rear view mirror, Raymond noticed a New Mexico Highway Patrol car trailing them.
13. The New Mexico Highway Patrol pulled them over when they reached Arizona.
14. The officers pulled Raymond over because of a defective rear end reflector.
15. The officer said two black males had robbed a bank in Albuquerque and were headed their way.
16. Raymond received two tickets; one for speeding and the other for a defective rear end reflector.
17. Being pulled over was nothing new to Milton; he was used to it.
18. The officers found open containers in the car.
19. The officers video taped the entire procedure.
20. Raymond's stepfather told the officers they should not judge black adolescents by the way they dressed or wore their caps.

PART II. Definitions
Use a dictionary to find the definitions of words listed below. Report your findings to the class. Discuss how the words were used in Chapter 16.

Abrupt	justifiable
accidentally	leg
Accordingly	maturity
Approximately	distinguish
Pride	distraction
satisfactorily	summoned
Prudent	

Part III. Raymond's Route to California

Trace Raymond's route from home (Chicago) to UCLA (Los Angeles, California. Answer the following questions relating to the trip:

1. What is the name of the city and state where they spent the first night?

A. Albuquerque, New Mexico
B. Amarillo, Texas
C. Flagstaff, Arizona
D. Chicago, Illinois
E. Phoenix, Arizona
F. Los Angeles, California

What is the name of the second city and state where they spent the night?

3. The Arizona Highway Patrol pulled them over near what metropolitan city?
A. Los Angeles, California
C. Albuquerque, New Mexico
B. Flagstaff, Arizona
D. Amarillo, Texas

4. Slap Burgers signs were coming up pretty fast near what metropolitan city?
A. Chicago, Illinois
C. Flagstaff, Arizona
B. Phoenix, Arizona
D. Amarillo, Texas

PART V Discussion
Discuss the following questions. Be prepared to defend your answer with concrete examples.

  A. Did the highway patrol have justifiable reasons for stopping Raymond? Explain your answer.
  B. Do you think black male adolescents are treated fairly in the judicial system?
  C. Why did Raymond's stepfather tell Raymond and Milton to keep their hands visible?
  D. Why was Mrs. Tinsley concerned about Raymond's driving across country to California?

Class Project
Obtain a road map of the United States. Trace Raymond's route from Chicago to Los Angeles, California.
A. Locate the cities where they spent the night and the Interstate they used to get there.

UNIT IV TEST
Chapters 13-16

Name _____ Homeroom _____ Score _____

PART I. True/False (100 points)
1. _____ Coach Mickey was still in the hospital recovering from gunshot wounds.
2. _____ MLK lost to Carver in the state championship game
3. _____ Mrs. Tinsley told Raymond she would understand if he fell behind in his studies.
4. _____ Coach Mickey laughed so hard that he had to pretend he was choking on the chicken and beer.
5. _____ Gerald's partners were drug users.
6. _____ Gerald's partners remained at the party until it was over.
7. _____ Mr. Duncan was watching the Super Bowl Game in his van.
8. _____ Raymond never talked to Gerald about his drug problem.
9. _____ Gerald was a junior at Carver High School.
10. _____ Raymond knew that if Mrs. Tinsley had gotten upset with Gerald, the neighborhood would know about it.
11. _____ Cassandra and Raymond had scholarships to the same college.
12. _____ Cassandra asked Raymond to meet her in front of Foot Locker.
13. _____ The two little girls who saw Raymond and Cassandra kissing told them to stop.
14. _____ Raymond told Dr. Healy he would attend the retreat.
15. _____ Raymond jumped out of the window after Cassandra told him to meet her at Foot Locker.
16. _____ They watched an X-rated movie.
17. _____ Cassandra was leaving for college the next Friday.
18. _____ Two people were wounded in the cross-fire.
19. _____ On the way home, Raymond and Cassandra talked about the flight to California.
20. _____ Cassandra and Raymond realized the urgency of stopping kids from killing kids.
21. _____ After dropping Cassandra off at home, Raymond called Milton on his cell phone.
22. _____ The boys decided to fmd out more about the prevention and intervention program at Jesse Owens Park.
23. _____ They picked up Eric Malone on the way to the park.
24. _____ Jeffrey Cunningham played ball with Milton's brother for MLK High School.
25. _____ Jeffrey Cunningham was a senior at Malcolm X High School.
26. _____ When they arrived at the park, they located Jeffrey at a staff meeting.
27. _____ The staff consisted only of black male college students.
28. _____ The three boys left the park learning very little about the prevention and intervention program.

29. _____ Before the program, 70% of the clients felt that gang activities would increase.
30. _____ After the program started, 28% felt that gang activities would increase.
31. _____ Only Raymond agreed to work in the prevention and intervention program.
32. _____ The gangs established a dialogue through sports.
33. _____ A truce was declared while participating in park activities.
34. _____ Before leaving for college, Raymond wanted to spend his time with the prevention and intervention program.
35. _____ Adolescents participating in an activity they enjoy are less likely to destroy property or themselves.
36. _____ Raymond told Dr. Healy he would attend the weekend retreat.
37. _____ The program at Jesse Owens Park was a model for other parks.
38. _____ Thoughts and feelings about the little girl wounded in the crossfire would not go away.
39. _____ Raymond and his mother agreed he would not take the car to college until he had satisfactorily completed his freshman year.
40. _____ Raymond knew he had to do well his freshman year.
41. _____ Raymond's stepfather felt Raymond would make the adjustment with or without a car.
42. _____ Driving across country was a major concern of Mrs. Tinsley.
43. _____ She only agreed to his taking the car after Raymond's stepfather said he would go along with the boys on the drive to California.
44. _____ Mrs. Tinsley and Milton's mother talked approximately two hours on the phone.
45. _____ The American Automobile Association mapped their routes and rest stops to California.
46. _____ Raymond drove the first leg of the trip.
47. _____ Sixteen hours after leaving home, they stayed overnight in Flagstaff, Arizona.
48. _____ Milton was snoring so hard that Raymond had to use his radio earphones.
49. _____ Raymond knew they were getting close to Los Angeles because fast food billboards were coming up pretty fast.
50. _____ In the rear view mirror, Raymond noticed a New Mexico Highway Patrol car trailing them.

Chapter Seventeen

An official apology from the City of Flagstaff
Flagstaff adopts prevention and intervention model
from Chicago
The co-ed dormitory
Milton falls asleep with his ear to the wall

Raymond falls asleep thinking about his first night on a college campus

At dusk, they were within Flagstaff's city limits. Raymond suggested they stop for food before checking into the motel. "We passed exit 22A. That was the Slap Burgers exit." Milton said.

"No Slap Burgers tonight. We are going to eat a real meal for a change. From what we have just gone through, I think we deserve a better meal." Raymond's stepfather said with a smile. "Old Country Buffet, All you can eat, 2 miles ahead, Exit 27B" (the billboard read). "Now that's my kind of eating establishment. Milton, if you want to get to Los Angeles, you had better not miss exit 27B."

Milton knew Raymond's dad was serious when it came to eating. In the buffet line, Raymond's dad-father selected fried chicken, sliced beef, meatballs, macaroni and cheese, spinach, and rice covered with gravy. The man could eat. They joked about his eating on the way to the hotel.

A black Flagstaff police officer pulled in behind them when they arrived at the Holiday Inn. "Oh sir," the policeman said walking toward them. "May I speak with you guys?" The first thing that came to their minds was the incident on the highway with the Arizona Highway Patrol. Was this another mistake of prejudging the character of black adolescents? The officer and a brother in plain clothes introduced themselves. "We knew you guys were on your way here. We received the information from the state highway patrol," he continued. "We are here to welcome you to Flagstaff and to personally apologize for the humiliating experience with the state police.

The city of Flagstaff has a program in place that clearly spells out how to not discriminate against black males. Ronald, my fellow officer here, is a part of that program."

"Good to meet you," Ronald said. "I know you guys are tired so go on and get some rest."

"It's good to meet you, too, brother," Raymond said.

"Hey Raymond, these officers need to hook-up with Jeffrey Cunningham," Milton said.

"Yeah, yeah! That's right. A friend of ours is directing a youth program at one of the park districts in Chicago. Get in touch with this brother. He has a good program for black males. I don't know the exact address, but I'm sure you can get the information by phone. That's Jeffrey Cunningham, Jesse Owens Park on west 87th Street, Chicago, Illinois." The officer wrote the information down and said good night.

The three checked into the Holiday Inn hoping to get a good night's rest Raymond's dad bought the Flagstaff Tribune and the they went to their rooms. On the front page was a picture of two little black girls hugging each other crying as their father lay in front of then,, shot: a victim of a drive-by shooting. The person suspected of committing the crime was an eleven year old gang member. On the most dangerous streets, guns aren't just used for survival and revenge; they are perceived as the ultimate power and authority. It used to be that only two or three gang members would have guns. Now they all have them.

The next morning, they were up early for that final leg to Los Angeles. At 7 p.m. they were in a traffic jam looking at the skyline of Los Angeles, California. Sitting in the back seat reading the city street map of Los Angeles, Milton gave directions to the university.

They arrived at John Wooden's co-ed dormitory at 8:15 p.m. Steve Barnes was sitting in the lobby waiting. Raymond had called from Flagstaff, giving Steve an approximate time for their arrival. Steve introduced Raymond and Milton to the dormitory staff and later showed them to their rooms. They passed several young ladies on the way to their rooms. They had to restrain Milton.

Milton, with girls living next door! This may not be a good idea, Raymond thought to himself.

"Don't get any ideas about this co-ed dorm. There are restrictions." Steve said jokingly. "The shuttle bus picked up your luggage. It should already be in your room."

Raymond and Milton later gave Raymond's dad a ride to the airport. He took the 12 o'clock red-eye express back to Chicago. When they arrived back at the dormitory, they were up until 3 a.m. talking about their cross-country trip. Before falling asleep, Milton placed his ear against the wall trying to hear what was going on in the girl's room next door.

"Milton, you are a crazy dude," Raymond said.

"Be cool, R.T., I think I hear something," Milton said.

Raymond fell asleep thinking about his first night on a college campus. Milton fell asleep with his ear to the wall!

Activities

Understanding what you have read.
Do not write in this book Use your Raymond Tinsley journal.

PART I. True/False
1. ____ Raymond's dad told Milton to take the Slap Burgers exit.
2. ____ They all had Slap Burgers and fries.
3. ____ Raymond's dad ate two Slap Burgers.
4. ____ The officer told Raymond the City of Flagstaff would continue to discriminate against black males.
5. ____ Milton knocked on the wall to get the girls attention.
6. ____ Raymond told Milton to go knock on the door.
7. ____ They stayed up until 3 a.m. talking about the trip across-country.
8. ____ They dropped Raymond's dad off at the Greyhound bus station.
9. ____ Raymond fell asleep with his ear to the wall.
10. ____ Milton fell asleep thinking about his first night on a college campus.

PART II. Completions
Fill in each blank with the correct word from the list below to complete the sentence.
1. At dusk, they were within the city limits of _____
2. "We passed exit 22B. That was the _____ exit."
3. A _____ police officer pulled up behind them.
4. Flagstaff has a program in place that clearly spells out how not to _____ against black males.
5. The humiliating experience happened with the _____
6. They arrived at _____ dormitory at 8:15 p.m.
7. _____ was waiting in the lobby.
8. Steve Barnes told Milton there were _____ living in a co-ed dormitory.
9. Milton fell asleep with his _____ to the wall.
10. Raymond's dad took the 12 o'clock red-eye express back to - Arizona High way Patrol

John Wooden's coed dormitory
black
Flagstaff, Arizona
discriminate
Chicago
restrictions
Slapburgers
Steve Barnes
Ear

PART III Vocabulary

Use a dictionary to find the definition of the words listed below. Construct a new sentence for each word. Explain how the word was used in Chapter 17.

Authority	dormitory
perceived	restrictions
Buffet	establishment
power	shuttle
Discriminate	obtain
restrain	ultimate

PART IV Writing Prompts

A. Why do you think the officer told Raymond's stepfather, Raymond and Milton they had a program in place to not discriminate against black males?

B. If you had the money and resources, how would you use them to stop gang violence?

C. How do you think eleven year old boys obtain guns?

Chapter Eighteen

The drive-through registration
Raymond knows he has to go to another level of play to run with this team
Visible gang signs on abandoned buildings
R.T., the five-second play

A breathless moment for Cal State fans

Steve Barnes was the point man working with incoming freshmen athletes. Today, he was assisting them with registering and scheduling classes. Ring! Ring!! The phone at a level loud enough to awaken Raymond and Milton was insistently ringing in their ears. Steve Barnes was calling to remind them he would be there at 10 a.m. Raymond had practically forgotten about registration and getting their fall class schedule.

After talking with Steve, Raymond and Milton showered, got dressed, and prepared for their second day on campus. When they reached the registration area, there were long lines of students registering for classes. "Man, I hope we don't have to get at the end of one of those lines." Milton said.

"No, my brother," Steve said, "I know a few short cuts through this madness." Steve stopped at the director's office. After a few minutes with the director he emerged carrying a basket containing several registration packets. Steve and the athletes went into a room adjacent to the director's office. Each packet had one of the athletes' name and Coach Reeves name on it. They signed the required forms and got their fall classes in approximately ten minutes.

Raymond knew this was too easy. Coach Reeves probably had something to do with this cruise through registration. Maybe we are being treated like VIP's because we are from Chicago, Raymond thought... No way!

After registration, Coach Reeves wanted to meet with the freshmen athletes. When they arrived at the gym, the varsity team was in full practice. After a few minutes of watching them practice, Raymond knew he had to go to another level of play to run with this team.

Coach Reeves blew the whistle to end the practice. The team walked over and introduced themselves. "Okay, okay, so much for salutations," coach said. "Are you guys staying for my meeting?" he asked the varsity team. The varsity team agreed to stay; some of them wanted to talk to Raymond and Clarence (The Hook). The Hook had been on campus four days. He had attended the retreat for freshmen athletes.

Coach Reeves spoke of team goals, expectations of each athlete, and how to develop a winning attitude in sports and academics. After the meeting, they toured the fitness center. Male and female athletes used the facility. Full time instructors were there to assist athletes in developing their physical skills. It was really high class and high tech.

Raymond could see that the competition was going to be stiff. He knew he had to spend some time in this facility if he was going to run with the varsity team. Before he had been the star player, now he was just a member of a team made up of other star players. But it was also a wonderful opportunity.

After the tour, Coach Reeves gave each player a copy of the practice schedule. In addition to practice, six hours a week in the fitness room were required. The first practice was to be tomorrow from 4 to 7 p.m. Both Milton and Raymond were used to working out and hard work and really looked forward to their first session.

The first six weeks of college went without a hitch for the boys. They began practicing for their road games. Neither Raymond nor Milton had flown before; other than at the state fair where they paid ten dollars each to take a fifteen minute ride in a helicopter.

The Hook had flown on several occasions when visiting his aunt in Detroit, Michigan.

Steve Barnes told the boys it wouldn't take long for them to get used to flying. Raymond thought, now you speak for yourself. He was very quiet on the way to the airport. He didn't want the team to know he was a little apprehensive about his first flight.

After they were airborne for the flight to the University of California, Berkeley, they flew into bad weather. It was a bumpy ride all the way. Milton almost had an accident before they landed in Oakland. They boarded the bus for the forty minute ride to the university. From the bus, the boys got a good view of Oakland's inner city.

Black male adolescents congregated on the streets. Gangs signs were visible on vacant buildings. Gang signs are indications of social problems and issues facing black adolescents growing up and attending inner city schools. Raymond realized that inner-city black adolescents needed more effective programs like the one Jeffrey Cunningham directs for this generation of black adolescents to survive.

After lunch, they had two hours of free time on campus. The coach emphasized 'on campus.' They walked around the beautiful campus of the University of California at Berkeley. Milton stopped a foreign black student who spoke very little English. She understood very little of what Milton was saying; the girl appeared to be in shock. She accidentally dropped her book bag in a trash basket standing near her. Milton was laying a heavy rap. Relief came only when Raymond told Milton it was time to make it to the gym. They left the fine sister standing in the middle of the pathway, startled by her experience with Milton. Lifting her book bag out of the trash basket, she continued to look at Milton until they were out of view, thinking about his conversation with her.

"Man! What did you say to that sister?" Raymond asked.

"I told her I loved her at first sight, and wanted to marry her before I leave campus."

"Man, you are one crazy dude! One of these days these idle promises are going to catch up with you," Raymond said jokingly.

The boys returned to the visiting team quarters to prepare for the game. Raymond, Milton, and The Hook were on the floor an hour before the team arrived going through routines from the game plan. At 7:58 p.m., the horn blew for the start of the game between UCLA and Cal State University, Berkeley. Cal

Chapter Eighteen

State ranked as the best defensive team in the southwest conference. UCLA was a fast pace team with an explosive offense.

At half time, Cal State was leading by eight points: 42-34. At the end of the third quarter, Cal State was ahead by six points. Coach Reeves attempted a variety of offenses, but the defensive team wouldn't let up. Raymond, Milton, and The Hook had only played briefly in the first half. Coach Reeves stayed with the starting five until the last three minutes of the game. Time-out was called by UCLA with 2:53 showing on the clock. UCLA was down seven points. The Coach knew they were going to lose the game unless something drastically fired up his offense. He called on the boys from Chicago: Raymond, Milton, and The Hook. "All right," Milton said, "let's play some Chicago ball!"

"Let's play some Chicago ball!" echoed The Hook. The boys from Chicago immediately took the fans of Cal State out of the game. The Hook was hooking.

The alley-oops to Raymond under the baskets, and two three point shots by Milton tied the score with twelve seconds remaining on the shot clock.

"Time-out, Cal State. After the time-out, a foul was called on The Hook. "Shooting one on one," the referee shouted. The Cal State player missed the first shot but made the second. "Time-out, UCLA. With six seconds remaining on the clock, Cal State - 71, UCLA - 70!" the announcer shouted.

"R.T., R.T.," Milton shouted.

"What is R.T.," the coach asked.

"R.T. is a five second play we used to win the city championship with last year," Milton answered.

How well The Hook remembered the play. It was the last play used to beat Carver. The boys had practiced this play regularly.

"Okay, lets go with it!" shouted the coach. A quick pass in from the UCLA forward to Milton, a pass to The Hook above the heads of the Cal State defenders, and an alley-oop to Raymond under the basket. Raymond faked a jump shot, then he came in like thunder from the left side of the basket and dunked the shot over his back for the winning points. The popping of the nets sent a piercing sound to the ears of Cal State fans. The red plastic covering the exit sign shattered into little pieces and fell to the floor. It was a breathless moment for Cal State fans. They were speechless after witnessing the athletic performance of the boys from Chicago. The fans quietly left the arena trying to figure out what had happened.

The team talked about the play during the return flight to Los Angeles. Coach Reeves knew he had to make some changes in his starting five after what happened tonight.

Activities

Understanding what you have read
Do not write in this book. Use your Raymond Tinsley journal

PART I *Discussions*
A. What signs did Raymond see in Oakland indicating black adolescents are facing social problems similar to those in other cities?
B. Why do you think Raymond stated we need more programs like the one Jeffrey Cunningham directs? *Give reasons for your explanation.*

PART II *Class Project*
A. Call city hall for gang awareness information.
B. Ask what communities are doing to stop gang violence
C. Contact the department of Human Resources for data on gang violence. Report your findings to the class.

PART III True/False
1. Steve Barnes called Milton and Raymond to remind them of registration for fall classes.
2. Steve Barnes was the point man working with incoming freshmen athletes.
3. When they reached the registration area, the lines were relatively short.
4. Steve told the boys it would probably take all day to register for fall classes.
5. When they arrived at the gym, the varsity team was on a break.
6. They all left before Coach Reeves started the meeting with the freshmen.
7. The boys were required to workout twelve hours a week in the fitness room.
8. Full time instructors were available to assist the boys in the fitness room.
9. The foreign student clearly understood what Milton was saying to her.
10. Gang signs on vacant buildings, black adolescents congregating were indications of social problems in the community.
11. Raymond realized that black adolescents in Oakland needed programs like the one Jeffrey Cunningham directs.
12. The Hook had flown on several trips to visit his uncle in Detroit.
13. Cal State was ranked as the best offensive team in the southwest conference.
14. UCLA was a fast paced team with an explosive offense.
15. UCLA lost by two points.

PART IV. Definitions

Use a dictionary to find the definition of words from the Word Bank listed below. Report your findings to the class.

Approximately	relatively
breathless	retreat
Director	salutations
emerge	shattered
Foreign	speechless
hitch	piercing
Apprehensive	registration
packet	varsity

The RAYMOND TINSLEY Story
Get Up On The Hook

Willie Hoskins

Chapter Nineteen

The boys return to Chicago for the summer
More about the prevention and intervention program
A clinic conducted by athletes from the NBA
A dialogue with gangbangers, NBA athletes, college athletes, and community leaders

The boys from Chicago outswim the sharks

The UCLA basketball team made it to NCAA finals, but lost to Washington State in the third round. After completing an exciting year, the boys returned to Chicago for the summer. Raymond's dad flew to California and drove back with them. Raymond slept-in the first two days. He called Jeffrey Cunningham at the park to find out more about the prevention and intervention program.

"Hey! Raymond, I'm glad you called. We are putting together a summer basketball clinic and tournament," Jeffrey said.

Raymond talked to Milton and Clarence and they agreed to meet at the park the next day to see about participating in the summer program. The clinic was conducted by professional players from the National Basketball Association. With combined talent from the NBA and college athletes, the program attracted gangbangers from all over the city. Not only did sports keep the truce between the gangs, but a dialogue between the different gang factions; dialogue between the gangs, college athletes, NBA players, and community leaders were key factors. Weekly, all factions came together and discussed social problems and emotional issues of adolescents growing up and attending inner city schools. Kids six through seventeen participated in the clinic and basketball tournament. Milton, Raymond, and Clarence each coached one of the little league basketball teams.

The success of Jeffrey Cunningham's program made national news. Cities across the country adopted programs similar to the one at Jesse Owens Park.

Two years before the program started, parents would not allow their children to play in the park because of gang activities. After two years in the program, children were returning to the park. Gang activities were down to a fraction of what they used to be. Gang activities took a nose-dive after the successful clinic and tournament.

Raymond, Milton, and Clarence's participation in the program attracted out of state college athletes. Since the drive-by shooting of the little girl, Raymond knew he had to get involved with the social and emotional problems of black adolescents growing up and attending inner-city schools.

Two years before the program started, parents would not allow their children to play in the park because of gang activities. After two years in the program, children were returning to the park. Gang activities were down to a fraction of what they used to be. Gang activities took a nose-dive after the successful clinic and tournament.

The boys continued working with the summer youth program during their sophomore and junior years at UCLA. August would always roll around pretty fast. This August they were preparing for their senior year at UCLA. Raymond's father really looked forward to this time of year because he got to drive with the boys back to California.

The boys from Chicago continued to amaze people wherever they played. Scouts from the NBA were now taking a close look at Raymond, Milton, and Clarence. The Detroit Pistons wanted to sign all three of them. It appeared as if they knew where each other were on the court at all times. Professional sports writers predicted this is the year UCLA would win the national championship.

Twenty games into the season, UCLA was undefeated. Arizona State came close on their home court, but the boys from Chicago put on a show to pull it out for UCLA.

The game against the University of Honolulu, in Honolulu, Hawaii was an experience the boys would never forget. On the return flight home, the plane had to fly around a hurricane in the Pacific Ocean. The team sat quietly as the pilots tried to maneuver the aircraft through the turbulent weather.

"Man, this is a bumpy ride. I hope the pilot has it under control," Clarence said.

"Yeah, me too," Milton answered. Raymond was sitting at the front of the aircraft with the coach talking about the upcoming drafts of college athletes. The plane was losing altitude each time it hit an air pocket. Everyone on the plane stopped talking after the pilot turned on the emergency light and asked passengers to fasten their seat belts.

"Ladies and gentlemen, this is your pilot speaking. We are momentarily experiencing bad weather. We are going to take a detour around this storm because of its intensity. Please do not move around the aircraft until we turn off the emergency lights. I assure you, everything is okay up here and we should be coming out of the storm within the next twenty minutes," he explained.

Making a descending right turn, the lights went off in the aircraft. A loud explosion was heard near the rear of the craft. "May Day! May Day! Request location!" the pilot urgently called out over the intercom. The oxygen masks and survival kits fell from the upper compartment over each passenger's seat. Cabin attendants were frantically trying to keep everyone calm. Wobbling, followed by a trail of black smoke, the aircraft descended toward the Pacific Ocean waiting below.

The captain and crew did an outstanding job of landing the jumbo jet along the coast line of a small island in the Pacific. Looking out the window, Raymond noticed the coast line about a thousand yards away from the aircraft.

Life preservers were passed to passengers as water slowly filtered into the cabin. Raymond, Milton, and Clarence, calm and on top of things as usual, helped the cabin attendants. Some passengers received bumps and bruises during the emergency landing, but there were no serious injuries. The water slowly seeping into the cabin was now up to the plane's windows.

Chapter Nineteen

The captain told the passengers, the aircraft would remain afloat for eighteen hours. Because he was not sure if his radio transmission had been received and if they could depend on help coming any time soon, he asked if someone could swim ashore for help. As expected, the boys from Chicago volunteered for the mission.

Then Raymond, Milton, and Clarence changed into their basketball uniforms to make the thousand yard swim. They were glad they had learned to swim at the Better Boys Club back home. The weather was clear here and the water was calm, but swimming in the ocean was a new experience for the them. Fortunately, there were no hidden currents or undertow. But fifty yards from shore, a great white shark began trailing Milton.

"Milton! Milton!" Raymond shouted, "look out behind you." Simultaneously, as Milton looked back, a red flare penetrated the water between Milton and the shark. The flare gun shot came from the captain standing on the wing of the sinking plane as he watched the boys swim for help. Fortunately, the flare distracted the shark and it took off in another direction. When they reached the shore, they heard sounds of birds and other inhabitants of the island.

"Are you scared, man?" Raymond asked Milton.

"Yes!" he shouted.

"Aw man, this is like Robinson Crusoe and Friday. Remember they were trapped on an island somewhere in the Pacific until. . . ."

"Hey, I don't want to hear about it... I am scared." Milton said.

The boys walked about two miles inland until they came upon a clearing. A young native boy of the island was standing near by shouting, "A T M, A T M," just like the TV commercials. In the mainland those letters mean automatic teller machine. The native boy led Raymond, Milton, and Clarence to his village.

The village chief, a big formidable looking but friendly man, agreed to help rescue the stranded passengers. Hand crafted canoes were used to rescue the stranded passengers. Some passengers were outside standing on the wing of the plane when the boys returned to the sinking aircraft.

Luckily, the distress signal was picked up by a destroyer with the 6th Fleet before the aircraft went down. The ship's radar system pinpointed the exact location of the downed plane. The destroyer was en route to the small island to rescue the Americans. Passengers were standing on the beachhead waving to sailors as they approached the small island. They were transported to the destroyer by Chief Osukami (O-zoo-ka-me) and his crew. The rescue turned into a party. People were jamming with their CD's and cassettes. Some were doing the electric slide in the sand. The UCLA basketball team was seriously learning new dances: the Butterfly and Tootsie Roll. Before leaving, the passengers thanked Chief Osukami and his people for helping them.

The boys from Chicago were hailed as heroes. The heroic efforts of the boys from Chicago were the talk of the ship between passengers and sailors on the trip back to the states.

On their arrival, UCLA students, relatives and loved ones of the crash victims, the mayor of Los Angeles and well wishers were there to greet them. Television networks around the world carried the daring story of the rescue by the boys from Chicago.

Some newspaper's headlines read:

BOYS FROM CHICAGO OUTSWIM SHARKS
HEROIC RESCUE BY BOYS FROM CHICAGO
HIGH FIVE'S FOR THE 3 C'S

The news media ran away with the story. One tabloid magazine published a picture of Raymond kissing one of the native girls. One newspaper wrote: "The Boys from Chicago Swam Three Miles in Shark Infested Waters!" After two days of television interviews and talking to the news media, they finally resumed their lives as basketball players and students at UCLA.

Activities

Understanding what you have read.
Do not write in this book Use your Raymond Tinsley journal.

PART I. True/False
1. The UCLA basketball team made it to the NCAA fmals, but lost to Arizona State in the third round.
2. Completing an unsatisfactory freshmen year, Raymond had to attend summer school.
3. Raymond, Clarence, and Milton agreed to meet at the park to find out more about the prevention and intervention program. The program attracted gangbangers from all over the city.
4. The program was conducted by professional athletes from the NBA and Ages six through seventeen participated in the clinic but not the tournament.
5. Before the tournament, parents would not allow their kids to play in the park.
6. The success of Jeffrey Cunningham's program made national news.
7. NBA players, gang members, college students, and community leaders met weekly to discuss social issues and problems of adolescents growing up and attending inner-city schools.
8. Gang activities took a nose-dive after the successful clinic and tournament.
9. Raymond, Clarence, and Milton's participation in the program attracted college athletes from all over the United States.
10. After the drive-by shooting of the little girl, it was clearly decided by Raymond he had to get involved with the social issues and problems of adolescents growing up and attending inner-city schools.
11. The boys continued working with the youth program during their sophomore and junior years at UCLA.
12. The boys from Chicago continued to amaze people with their athletic performances wherever they played.
13. Scouts from the NBA were now taking a close look at the boys from Chicago.
14. The Detroit Pistons wanted to sign all three.
15. Twenty games into the season, UCLA was unbeaten.
16. Professional sports writers predicted Arizona State would win the National Championship.
17. The captain tried to maneuver the aircraft through the eye of the hurricane.
18. The plane gained altitude each time it hit an air pocket.
19. Raymond was sitting in the front of the plane talking to Cassandra Hawkins.
20. The plane crashed two hundred yards off-shore.
21. The captain told the passengers the plane would remain afloat for three days.
22. Someone had to swim ashore for help. The boys from Chicago volunteered for the mission.
23. The boys changed into their basketball sweats to make the swim to shore.
24. They learned to swim at the Better Boys Club in Chicago.
25. The only thing they could hear when they reached shore was the sound of birds.

26. They walked four miles inland until they came upon a clearing.
27. A young native boy was standing nearby shouting Automatic Teller Machines!
28. The village chief said he would not risk the lives of his people to rescue the stranded passengers.
29. Village-built canoes were used to rescue the passengers.
30. Some passengers were standing on the wing of the plane when the boys returned.
31. The distress signal was picked up by the radar of a passenger ship.
32. A U.S. Naval ship was already en route to rescue the stranded Americans.
33. The passengers were transported to the ship by Chief Osukami and his canoe party.
34. The rescue mission turned into a party.
35. Passengers were jamming with their cassettes and CD players.
36. Some were doing the Electric Slide in the sand.
37. The UCLA basketball team was seriously trying to learn new dances: the Butterfly and the Tootsie Roll.
38. They honored Chief Osukami and his people for helping the stranded passengers.
39. The heroic efforts of the boys from Chicago were the talk of the ship on the trip back to the states.
40. Chief Osukami and some of his people accompanied the team and passengers back to the states.
41. Television networks around the world carried the daring rescue story by the boys from Chicago.
42. One newspaper's headline read: "Boys from Chicago Out-Swam Sharks."
43. One tabloid published picture of Clarence kissing a native girl
44. After two days of interviews, the boys were invited to the White House.
45. The team took a two week vacation after returning to the states.
46. Raymond flew back to Chicago for a special interview.
47. Raymond said he would never fly again.
48. After two days of television interviews, the boys resumed their lives as basketball players and students at UCLA.

Chapter Nineteen

Activities cont.   Chapter 19

Part II. <u>Using Your Skills</u>

Jesse Owens Park provides year-round recreational activities for neighborhood kids. The most popular sport at the park is organized girls' and boys' basketball. Many kids do not participate in recreational activities in and near the park. Using the graph below, indicate the gain and loss of kids participating in recreational activities and in gang activities, in and near the park, before and after the clinic and tournament. Circle the correct answer.

A. Approximately how many girls participated in recreational activities at the park before the clinic and tournament?

(1) 45	(2) 25	(3) 35	(4) 40

B. Approximately how many boys participated?

(1) 55	(2) 75	(3) 70	(4) 180

C. How many kids participated in gang activities in and near the park before the clinic and tournament?

(1) 35	(2) 70	(3) 180	(4) 30

D. How many kids participated in gang activities after the clinic and tournament?

(1) 40	(2) 55	(3) 30	(4) 160

E. What is the difference in numbers of kids participating in gang activities before and after the clinic and tournament?

(1) 140	(2) 155	(3) 150	(4) 160

KIDS PARTICIPATING IN RECREATIONAL ACTIVITIES IN THE PARK BEFORE AND AFTER THE BASKETBALL CLINIC AND TOURNAMENT

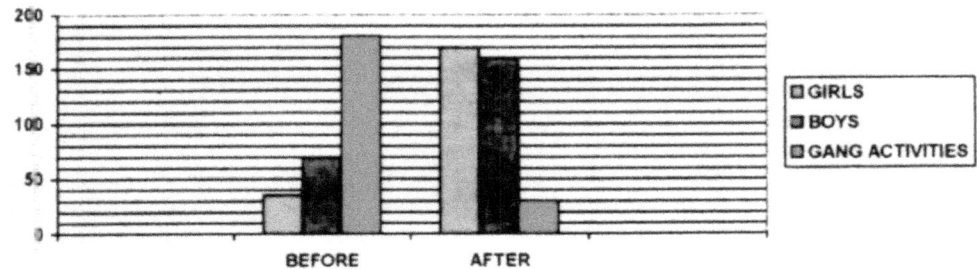

Part III Vocabulary
Use a dictionary to find the definition of the words listed below. Construct a new sentence for each word. Explain how the words were used in Chapter 19

Clinic	heroic
intercom	momentarily
Destroyer	infested
issues	predicted
Drafts	inhabitants
maneuver	preservers
Formidable	intensity
mission	stranded

Part IV. Writing Prompts
A. Describe Raymond and Milton's heroic swim in shark infested waters.
B. Would you have made the swim? Defend your answer.
    After reading Chapter 19, write a composition explaining why you think kids were returning to the park. Support your theory by using the data from the participation chart.

Chapter Twenty

The five-year, $30 million contract with the Chicago Bulls
"I may have contracted the HIV virus"

Raymond's family flew the red-eye express from Chicago to see Raymond receive his degree in Aeronautical Engineering from UCLA. Besides Raymond's mother, stepfather, his neighbor Mr. Duncan, his brother Gerald and his girl also attended the commencement exercises. Mrs. Tinsley could not hold back the tears watching Raymond receive his degree. She had lived for this day. She had prayed many nights for this to happen.

Cassandra Hawkins, the fine gymnast, also received her degree from Pepperdine University. She received her degree two days earlier than Raymond and was able to attend his graduation too.

After the graduation exercises, they decided to go out for dinner. They had a lot to celebrate. Not only had Raymond completed a difficult course of study to earn his degree while pursuing a career as an athlete, but Raymond, Milton, and Clarence were the first round draft picks of the NBA: Raymond to the Chicago Bulls, Milton to the Detroit Pistons, and Clarence to the Cleveland Cavaliers.

They were indecisive about choosing a place to eat. Raymond's stepfather interrupted saying he knew the perfect restaurant for dinner. Simultaneously they chorused "WHERE?"

"The original Slap Burgers Restaurant," he shouted with a big moon smile. Slowly, Mrs. Tinsley turned to him shaking her head with a definite "NO" expression on her face. How well they remembered the Slap Burgers franchise in Chicago and their famous burgers. But this was a special occasion. "No, Dad," Raymond said, we are going to a sit down restaurant.

"But wait, let me explain," he answered. "Los Angeles is the birthplace of Slap Burgers. I read about it in the March issue of Ebony Magazine.

They now serve gourmet food with valet parking. The Slap Burger dish is a specialty at the restaurant. Plus, they have live entertainment."

After a serious discussion, they agreed to go to Slap Burgers.

The restaurant had three levels. They chose a table down front on the third level. In the center of the restaurant was a revolving stage featuring live entertainment. When they reached the table, a young man wearing a Marine uniform and a young lady were already seated at the table.

"I. . . uh, uh. . . is that Curtis?" Raymond exclaimed. No, man, that couldn't be Curtis. Man! It is Curtis!"

Curtis got up from the table and they embraced each other in a brothers' hug. Seated at the table, also, was Evelyn (Dee Dee). The last time Raymond remembered seeing Dee Dee was in her apartment when they found her kids playing with a cigarette lighter near the curtains. Evelyn had completely turned her life around after that. She had gotten off drugs and into a program so she could go back to school and get her GED. She and Curtis had also gotten back together and were busy planning for the future. Mrs. Tinsley almost blacked out after discovering it was Curtis seated at the table. Raymond's stepfather was busy fanning her with a dinner napkin taken from a nearby table. Raymond's stepfather and Curtis had planned the whole thing. After settling down from the surprise appearance of Curtis, they had dinner and sat through two performances.

Returning to Chicago after graduation, Raymond reported to the Bulls organization for the required physical examination. He reportedly was signing a five year contract worth over $30,000,000 (thirty million dollars). He also had on the table, a $3,000,000 (three million dollar) advertising endorsement with Nike Sportswear.

Raymond's signing with the Chicago Bulls made the front page with The Chicago Defender, The Chicago Tribune and The Chicago Sun Times. Some stories read:

THE RETURN OF R.T. TO THE BIG C
HOMETOWN ROOKIE SIGNS WITH BULLS
PLANNING FOR THE MILLENIUM: BULLS SIGN R.T.

An article from The Chicago Defender read:

THE CHICAGO BULLS
PLANNING FOR THE MILLENIUM

The Chicago Bulls announced on Thursday they will sign Raymond Tinsley to a five year $230,000,000 contract. Sources tell The Chicago Tribune that the star center from UCLA will receive a 21.5 million signing bonus with built-in incentives from Nike Sportswear.

Raymond is a Chicago native who played local ball at Martin Luther King High School. Raymond was instrumental in helping to capture a local drug dealer during the city championship with Carver High School in 1996. In addition to his athletic talent, he spent his summers and school breaks working with inner city youth at Jesse Owens Park.

The Bulls Organization feels that he will not only help the team but will be a great role model for Chicago youth.

Clarence Johnson, The Hook, was reportedly signing a fat three-year, multi- million dollar contract for over $117,000,000 with a built-in performance clause worth $20,000,000 configuring points scored per season. His agent was asking for more. Clarence and Raymond were waiting to hear from Milton about his signing with the Detroit Pistons.

A week passed before hearing from him. Ring, Ring, Ring. Finally, "Hello," Mrs. Tinsley answered.

",Hi, Mrs. Tinsley, this is Milton. Is the millionaire there?"

"Milton, I am so glad you called. Raymond and Clarence were wondering why they hadn't heard from you."

"They are still negotiating my contract. It may take another week." he explained.

Chapter Twenty

"Well, Raymond and Cassandra went out to dinner. Is there a number where you can be reached?"

"Area code 746-947-5378. I am staying at the Hyatt Hilton in downtown Detroit. Tell him to call me at this number when he arrives."

"Let me see if I got the number right!" and she repeated the number back to him.

"That's right," Milton answered.

"Nice hearing from you, and take care of yourself."

"You too Mrs. Tinsley, good night!"

Later that evening Raymond returned Milton's phone call. "Hello, Milton Jones speaking."

"Milton, R.T. here. What's up, homie?"

"Hey man, we are still trying to put the deal together. My agent is driving a hard bargain. I will be back in Chicago tomorrow morning. Can you pick me up at the airport at 11:30?" Milton asked.

"Hey, no trouble!" Raymond responded happily, being glad to hear from his friend.

"I'm coming by Northeast Airlines"

"Okay, see you there."

The next morning, Raymond picked Milton up at the airport. The traffic was backed up on the Kennedy from O'Hare Airport for three miles. This gave the players a chance to talk about their contract signings.

"Hey man, the reason I didn't stay in touch was I haven't received the okay from my physical. My blood count was irregular, and they are still running tests. To be very truthful, R. T., I may have contracted the virus. "Milton said.

"Aw, man, I don't believe that. It could be a thousand other things. Professional basketball is a strenuous game. I think they want to be sure there are no foreseeable physical problems before signing you. That's typical of all the clubs."

"I know, but I had to tell my best friend. I haven't said anything to anyone else yet. For the first time in my life, excluding my first airplane ride, I have never been scared like this before."

"Hey man, you are about to sign a contract worth millions. They want to be sure of their investment. Sports are now a business. Every NBA club wants the best for its money. This thing will blow over." Raymond tried to encourage him.

Taking the Dan Ryan Expressway south, the young men finally made it to Milton's house. After dropping him off, many thoughts ran through Raymond's mind about Milton. What if the test results proved to be positive? Would Milton be able to cope knowing he was infected with the HIV virus? Would he remain his best friend? How would his family deal with it? How would this affect his play in the NBA, knowing that his best friend might die from AIDS.

The End

To be continued

Activities

Understanding what you have read.
Do not write in this book Use your Raymond Tinsley journal.

PART I. True/False
1. Raymond's mother flew the red-eye express from Chicago to see him receive his degree.
2. Raymond received a Bachelor of Science Degree in Aeronautical Engineering.
3. Raymond, Clarence, and Milton were first round draft picks of the NBA.
4. Milton was drafted by the Chicago Bulls.
5. Raymond signed a five year contract worth over five million dollars with the Detroit Pistons.
    1. Clarence Johnson was reportedly signing a fat multi-million dollar contract with the Cleveland Cavaliers for $17,000,000 (seventeen million dollars) over three years with a built-in performance clause worth $7,000,000 (seven million dollars) based upon points scored per season. His agent was asking for more.
6. Clarence and Raymond were waiting to hear from Milton and his signing with the Detroit Pistons.
7. All three boys successfully passed the NBA physical.
8. Milton was staying at the Holiday Inn in Downtown Detroit.
9. Milton flew Northwest Airlines from Detroit.
10. Milton told Raymond he might have contracted the HIV Virus.

UNIT V TEST

FINAL EXAM

Name _____ Score _____
Grade _____ Homeroom _____ Date _____

PART I True/False (100 points)

_____ 1. Raymond's dad told Milton to take the Slap burgers exit.
_____ 2. They all had Slap burgers.
_____ 3. Raymond's dad ate two Slap burgers.
_____ 4. The officer told Raymond the City of Flagstaff would continue to Discriminate against black males.
_____ 5. Milton knocked on the wall to get the girls' attention.
_____ 6. Raymond told Milton to go knock on the door.
_____ 7. They stayed up until 3 a.m. talking about the trip across-country.
_____ 8. They dropped Raymond's dad off at the Greyhound bus station.
_____ 9. Raymond fell asleep with his ear to the wall.
_____ 10. Milton fell asleep thinking about his first night on a college campus.
_____ 11. Steve Barnes called Milton and Raymond to remind them of registration for fall classes.
_____ 12. Steve Barnes was the point man working with incoming freshman athletes.
_____ 13. When they reached the registration area, the lines were relatively short.
_____ 14. Steve told the boys it would probably take all day to register for fall classes.
_____ 15. When they arrived at the gym, the varsity team was on a break.
_____ 16. They all left before Coach Reeves started the meeting with the freshmen.
_____ 17. The boys were required to workout twelve hours a week in the fitnes room.
_____ 18. Full time instructors were available to assist the boys in the fitness room.
_____ 19. The foreign student clearly understood what Milton was saying to her.
_____ 20. Gang signs on vacant buildings and black adolescents congregating were indications of social problems in the community.
_____ 21. Raymond realized that black adolescents in Oakland needed programs like the one Jeffrey Cunningham directed.
_____ 22. The Hook had flown on several trips to visit his uncle in Detroit.
_____ 23. Cal State was ranked as the best offensive team in the southwest conference.
_____ 24. UCLA was a fast-paced team with an explosive offense.
_____ 25. UCLA lost by two points.
_____ 26. The UCLA basketball team made it to the NCAA finals but lost to Arizona State in the third round.
_____ 27. Following an unsatisfactory freshman year, Raymond had to attend summer school.

_____ 28. Raymond, Clarence and Milton agreed to meet at the park to find out more about the prevention and intervention program.
_____ 29. The program attracted gangbangers from all over the city.
_____ 30. The program was conducted by college student-athletes and by professional athletes from the NBA.
_____ 31. Young people ages six through seventeen participated in the clinic but not the tournament.
_____ 32. Before the tournament, parents would not allow their kids to play in the park.
_____ 33. The success of Jeffrey Cunningham's program made national news.
_____ 34. NBA players, gang members, college students, and community leaders met weekly to discuss social issues and problems of adolescents growing up and attending inner-city schools.
_____ 35. Gang activities took a nose-dive after the clinic and tournament.
_____ 36. After the drive-by shooting of the little girl, it was clearly decided by Raymond that he had to get involved with the social issues and problems of adolescents growing up and attending inner-cityschools.
_____ 37. The boys continued working with the youth program during their sophomore and junior years at UCLA.
_____ 38. The boys from Chicago continued to amaze people with their athletic performances wherever they played.
_____ 39. Scouts from the NBA were now taking a close look at the boys from Chicago.
_____ 40. The Detroit Pistons wanted to sign all three.
_____ 41. Twenty games into the season, UCLA was undefeated.
_____ 42. Professional sports writers predicted that Arizona State would win the National Championship.
_____ 43. The captain tried to maneuver the aircraft through the eye of the hurricane.
_____ 44. The plane gained altitude each time it hit an air pocket.
_____ 45. Raymond was sitting in the front of the plane talking to Cassandra Hawkins.
_____ 46. The plane crashed two hundred yards off-shore.
_____ 47. The captain told the passengers the plane would remain afloat for three days.
_____ 48. Someone had to swim ashore for help. The boys from Chicago volunteered for the mission.
_____ 49. The boys changed into their basketball sweats to make the swim to shore.
_____ 50. They had learned to swim at the Better Boys Club in Chicago.
_____ 51. The only thing they could hear when they reached shore was the sound of birds.
_____ 52. They walked four miles inland until they came upon a clearing.
_____ 53. A young native boy was standing nearby shouting "Automatic Teller Machines!"
_____ 54. The village chief said he would not risk the lives of his people to rescue the stranded passengers.
_____ 55. Village-built canoes were used to rescue the passengers.
_____ 56. Some passengers were standing on the wing of the plane when the boys returned.
_____ 57. The distress signal was picked up by radar of a passenger ship.
_____ 58. A U.S. Naval ship was already en-route to rescue the stranded. Americans.
_____ 59. The passengers were transported to the ship by Chief Osukami and his canoe party.
_____ 60. The rescue mission turned into a party.

_____61. Passengers were jamming with their cassettes and CD players.
_____62. Some were doing the Electric Slide in the sand.
_____63. The UCLA basketball team was seriously trying to learn new dances: The Butterfly and the Tootsie Roll.
_____64. They honored Chief Osukami and his people for helping the stranded passengers.
_____65. The heroic efforts of the boys from Chicago were the talk of the ship on the trip back to the states.
_____66. Chief Osukami and some of his people accompanied the team and passengers back to the states.
_____67. Television net works around the world carried the daring rescue story by the boys from Chicago.
_____68. One newspaper's headline read: "Boys from Chicago Out-Swim Sharks."
_____69. One tabloid published a picture of Clarence kissing a native girl.
_____70. After two days of interviews, the boys were invited to the White House.
_____71. The team took a two-week vacation after returning to the states.
_____72. The team took a one-week vacation after returning to the states.
_____73. Raymond flew back to Chicago for a special interview.
_____74. Raymond said he would never fly again.
_____75. After two days of television interviews, the boys resumed their lives as basketball players and students at UCLA.
_____76. Raymond and his mother agreed he would not take the car to college until he satisfactorily completed his freshman year.
_____77. Raymond knew he had to do well his freshman year.
_____78. Raymond's stepfather felt Raymond would make the adjustment with or without the car.
_____79. Driving across country was a major concern for Mrs. Tinsley.
_____80. She only agreed to his taking the car after Raymond's stepfather said he would go with him.
_____81. Mrs. Tinsley and Milton's mother talked approximately two hours on the phone.
_____82. The American Automobile Association mapped their routes arid rest stops to California.
_____83. Raymond drove the first leg.
_____84. Sixteen hours after leaving home, they stayed overnight in Flagstaff, Arizona.
_____85. Milton was snoring so hard Raymond had to use his radio earphones.
_____86. Raymond knew they were getting close to Los Angeles; the fast food billboards were coming up pretty first.
_____87. In the rear view mirror, Raymond noticed a New Mexico Highway Patrol car trailing them.
_____88. The Highway Patrol pulled them over when they reached Arizona.
_____89. The officers pulled Raymond over because of a defective rear end reflector.
_____90. The officer said two black males had robbed a bank in El Paso and they were headed their way.
_____91. Raymond received two tickets: one for speeding and the other for a defective rear end reflector.
_____92. Being pulled over was nothing new to Milton; he was used to it.
_____93. The officers found open containers in the car.
_____94. The officers video taped the entire procedure.
_____95. Raymond's stepfather told the officers they should not judge black adolescents by the way they dressed or wore their caps.

_____ 96. Coach Mickey was still in the hospital recovering from the gunshot wounds.
_____ 97. MLK lost to Carver in the state championship game.
_____ 98. Mrs. Tinsley told Raymond she would understand if he fell behind in his studies.
_____ 99. Coach Mickey laughed so hard he had to pretend he was choking on the chicken and beer.
_____ 100. Gerald's partners were drug users.

Wilhos Publishing
P.O. Box 42369
Houston, Texas 77242
www.wilhospublishing.com

www.ingramcontent.com/pod-product-compliance
Lightning Source LLC
Chambersburg PA
CBHW081834300426
44116CB00014B/2583